This book belongs to
Jennifer MacFarlane.

AF477035

HISTORY OF EVERYDAY LIFE

HISTORY OF EVERYDAY LIFE

PIERO VENTURA

KINGFISHER BOOKS

First published in Great Britain in 1987 by KingfisherBooks Ltd
Elsley Court, 20–22 Great Titchfield Street, London W1P 7AD
A Grisewood & Dempsey Company

BRITISH LIBRARY CATALOGUING IN PUBLICATION DATA

Ventura, Piero
  Kingfisher history of everyday life.
  1. Manners and customs – History –
  Juvenile literature   2. Social history –
  Juvenile literature
  I. Title   II. Com'era una volta. *English*
  909   GT85

ISBN 0-86272-283-7

Typeset by Tradespools Ltd, Frome, Somerset
Printed and bound in Spain by Artes Graficas Toledo S.A
D.L.T.O. 1644–1986

Contents

Key

 Society, forms of government, institutions and economy

 Buildings, building techniques, architectural styles, city plans

 Cultivation of the land, work and lives of the peasants, food production

 Arts and crafts, the work of artisans and ordinary people, materials, techniques and products

 Exchange of goods, commercial life, lives of the merchants, markets and money

 Clothes, fashions and tastes

 Communications, means of transport, travel

 Inventions, technology and sources of energy

 Organization of the army and war tactics, the lives of soldiers, arms and armour

Introduction

We are often told that long ago there lived a powerful monarch, or that there was once a great poet, or in a far-off land there was an inventor. We are told about their high exploits, but we are told nothing about what many of us would really like to know – what their houses were like, or their towns, what sort of world they lived in, in fact just exactly how things used to be.

In history books we read about wars and battles, peasants and rulers, great artists and famous cities. Rarely do we hear about the details that make these things seem real – what people wore, how they travelled, where they lived and how they earned a living. If we had a more complete picture, perhaps we would be able to understand better why things happened the way they did, and what influenced leaders in making their decisions.

Imagine history to be like a giant knapsack that can be carried around. Each period of time, group of people, or place on the globe could be taken out and laid on the table. This book is a 'knapsack' – full of samples of the stories history has to offer. The readers dip into it to choose from among them.

Each chapter contains nine aspects of a particular era. Together they provide the reader with an overview of how life was at the time. Or the reader can choose particular subjects such as society, fashion, art and agriculture, and see how they differ over time and how important they were at every stage in history. So you can read this book in two ways: either as a guide to different periods in history, or as an introduction to various aspects of life through the ages.

Special topics discussed within each chapter are marked with symbols. These symbols are explained on the opposite page. The periods covered are introduced in the chapter title. A chart on page 159 shows where to find each subject at any given time in history.

# The Ancient World

Primitive nomadic tribes chose their chieftains for their courage, knowledge and ability to lead. These chiefs were familiar with the tribal gods, and able to guide their people by the stars. They also knew where to lead their tribes to find food and shelter. Because their constant search for food involved the whole tribe, no roles were assigned to any one individual or group, other than the women, who remained in the tents and cared for very young children.

Gradually, these wandering tribes settled in the fertile valleys of the great rivers, where they began to till the soil and build towns. In the Nile Valley, different groups which settled in Lower and Upper Egypt eventually united into a single kingdom ruled by *pharaohs*. The cities on the Tigris River and the Euphrates River also came under the control of

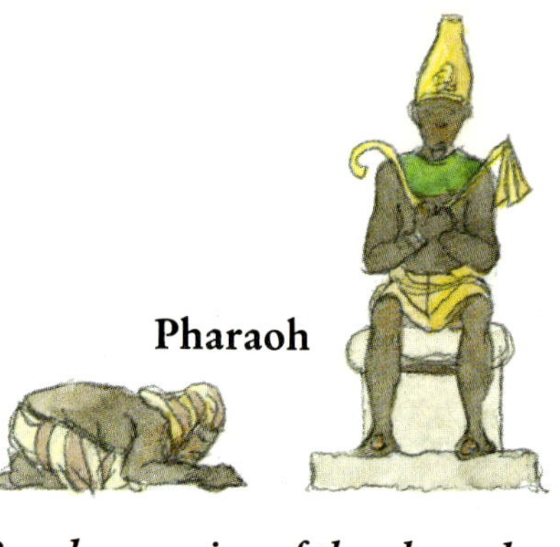

Pharaoh

Royal succession of the pharaoh was determined through the pharaoh's mother, who was believed to have conceived the pharaoh by the supreme god, Ammon. The role of 'divine woman' was then passed on to a daughter, often adopted, who in turn became the pharaoh's wife.

Priests

Soldiers

Various grades
of public servants
(civil servants)

In Egypt, showmen and merchants were considered special – the showmen because of their artistic talents, and the merchants because of their resourcefulness in travelling and establishing contacts in Asia and Africa.

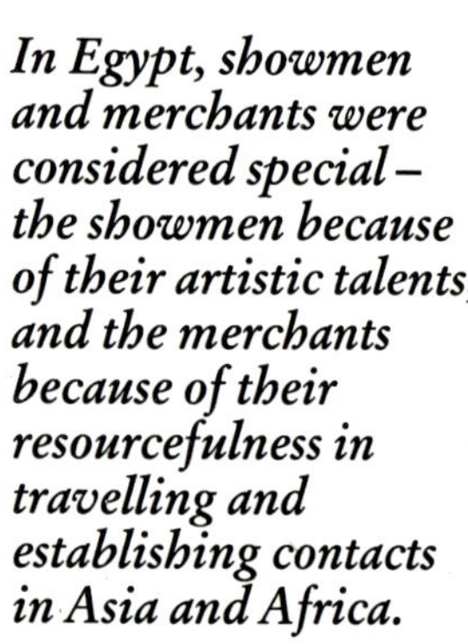

a single ruler, the Assyrian king Sargon II, while in Asia Minor the Hittite kings reigned. Western civilization as we know it was founded on these three great, ancient empires.

The social structure of these civilizations was, so people thought, ordained by the gods. The Egyptian pharaoh, like the kings of Babylon, represented the divinity. His reign was based on, and directed by, religious rituals. Priests were therefore a very powerful class, controlling not only these rituals, but the accession to the throne and the succession of the dynasties as well.

The army also held a key position in the state. It provided the force necessary to win and keep the king's position. Every soldier had to promise loyalty to the king, the supreme head of the armed forces. Equally important to the structure of the state were the civil servants. They ran the government and oversaw agricultural production, the state's main source of wealth.

Only the existence of huge numbers of slaves could support these 'non-productive' classes. Slave labour also made it possible for the state to build great monuments, the pyramids, palaces and temples of those ancient empires.

During the first thousand years BC, a new civilization with a different social structure, grew up on the shores of the Mediterranean in Greece. Unlike Egyptian rulers, no one man (except for certain Spartan monarchs, who held limited power) was able to unite all the city-states of ancient Greece into a single kingdom. Instead, the governments of these city-states were controlled by the wealthiest and most powerful families. These *aristocrats* formed councils to elect magistrates, such as the *archons* in Athens, who held power for a fixed period of time. In Athens in the fifth century BC, Pericles became the first aristocrat to introduce payment for administrative work. This meant that ordinary people could reach positions of power.

Women, who were excluded from all public life in 'democratic' Greece, were not even allowed to watch athletes compete in the Olympic games. Few people were truly free in Greece; the perioeci, *who were traders, and* helots, *who worked in the fields, were treated like slaves.*

9

Nomadic tribes, constantly on the move in search of food, lived in tents made of woven straw or animal skins which were easy to take apart and carry about. They would also shelter in caves or under trees, using weapons and fire to protect themselves from dangerous animals.

The nomadic tribes returned regularly to special sites. Perhaps these sites were places where their ancestors were buried or where they had placed a god's altar-stone. Perhaps they were places where they performed hunting and fertility rites. At these gatherings, goods were exchanged and marriages arranged. In time, the shrines and burial places where the tribes met, worshipped their gods, and bought and sold goods, became the nuclei of towns. In the centre were the two structures that embodied the tribe's history – the temple where the gods lived and the palace of the king.

Brick was the great invention of ancient builders. Whole cities were constructed of small, crude bricks made of clay that was baked in the sun. Great mounds of brick ruins which survive to this day hint at the grandeur of ancient Babylon.

The nomads, who gradually became herdsmen, found that migrating with herds and flocks was impossible. At first they sought pasturelands and then, as they became farmers, they settled in villages. The earliest houses were little more than huts, simple enclosures of rough stonework of straw mixed with dried mud, with roofs of matting and reeds supported by branches. The fire, which was usually outside the hut, was always kept alight, since it was so difficult to start up again if it went out. Settlements tended to grow up around rivers, springs or wells where there was a constant source of water. In Egyptian villages, the children played safely inside the walls while the women prepared food and drink, made jars to be used for storage, cut animal skins and wove fibres for clothes.

Animals were domesticated and given jobs to do. Oxen and camels were used for work; pigs kept the place clean by eating refuse. Cats and even snakes kept mice and other rodents away from food stored for the seasons in which crops could not be grown.

10

The gateway to the sacred enclosure
in an Egyptian temple

*The stone columns of
ancient Greece
imitated earlier
buildings that had
been supported by
wooden frames.
Because the Greeks
used stone, many of
their monuments are
still standing.*

The doorway of a Greek ionic style temple

A group of buildings made of mud and straw and bricks

*Cities with surrounding walls were safer to live in. However,
once people settled in cities, they found it harder to move
about freely. City life was therefore a departure from the
'freedom' of a nomadic way of life.*

Considering how old the human race is, the development of agriculture 10,000 years ago is relatively recent. The idea for sowing seeds probably came from noticing that plants always grew wherever seeds had fallen. Where groups of people stayed in one place for a time, they began to grow their own food nearby. It was certainly easier to grow their own grain and fruit than to be on a constant search for food.

The development of agriculture was a milestone in civilization. As agricultural techniques improved, more and more people could be fed and human's place in nature became more secure. The wealth of the ancient civilizations of the Mediterranean and the Near East was founded on agriculture.

Like everything else in these early societies, agriculture was controlled by the state. It claimed nearly all the farmers' produce, leaving them with barely enough food to survive. On the other hand, the state did much to encourage agriculture. They built canal systems to provide water for the crops to grow so that there would be enough produce to feed all the people.

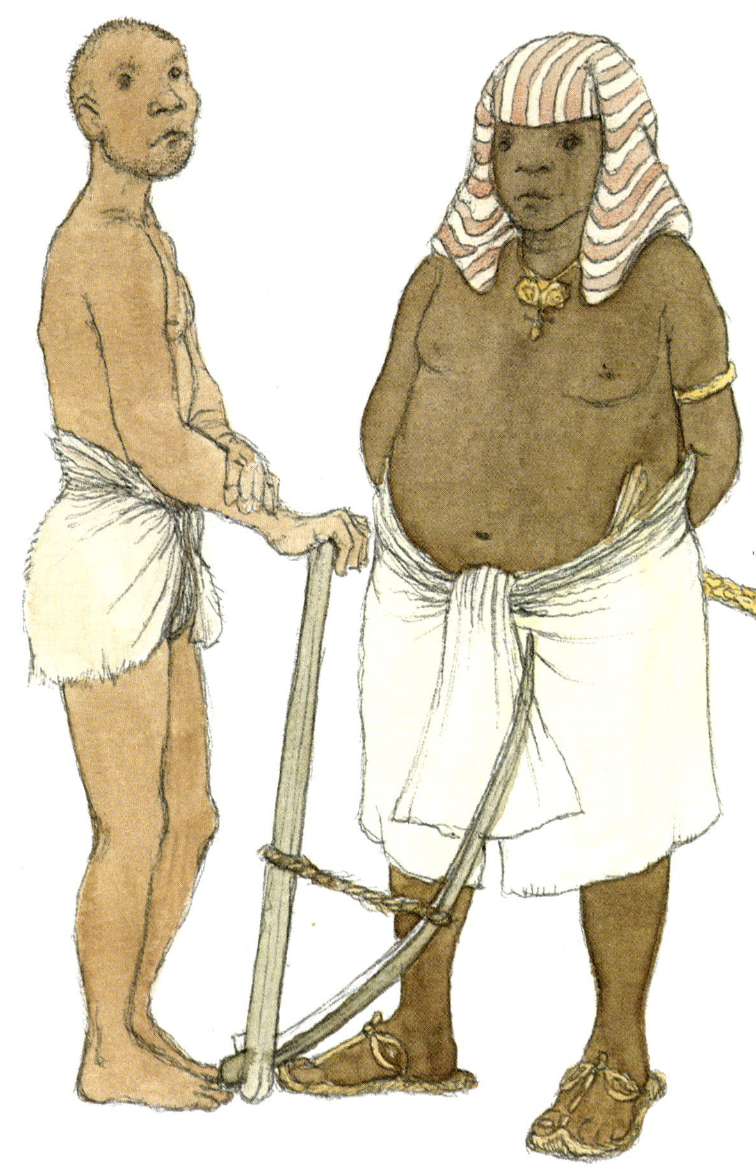

Farmer with a hoe and his Egyptian overseer

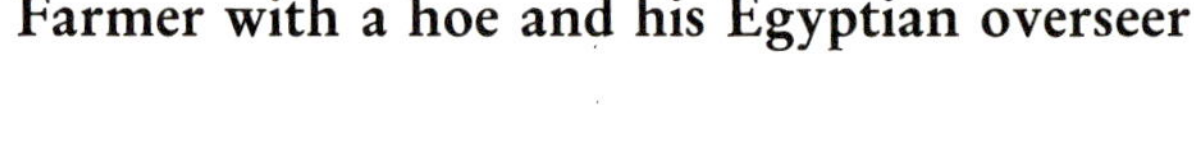

Prehistoric people, who realized that the land had to be tilled to be productive, invented first the hoe and then the plough. Because something larger and sharper than bare hands was needed to harvest crops, early rough flint tools were developed. These gradually changed to become the iron sickles that were used in Egyptian and Babylonian times.

Much of a woman's time was spent preparing and preserving food. Ancient Egyptian carvings show women baking bread and straining barley to make beer. Once animals were tamed and raised domestically, they were harnessed for pulling loads. Animals also became a source of wool, leather and food such as milk and eggs.

The regular flooding of the Nile carried fertile mud into the fields, guaranteeing two harvests a year. For irrigation, water had to be diverted from rivers and channelled through the fields. The Babylonians, expert hydraulic engineers, were very good at building irrigation systems. In less fortunate places, wells had to be dug and water drawn up in animal-skin buckets by means of a lever device called a shaduf, which is still used in Africa today.

13

We can learn a lot about the lives of ancient peoples from fragments of pottery. The ability to model and bake clay is one of mankind's oldest skills. The raw material is found almost everywhere. It is easy to shape and does not need to be baked at a high temperature.

The fine decoration and durability of a lot of ancient pottery suggest that potters must have been skilled and accomplished artists. The craftspeople who worked with more difficult materials such as metal must have been even more highly trained. Archaeological evidence shows that from the earliest times, craftspeople skilled in working with metal, clay, cloth, leather and dyes worked alongside the farmers, who made up the majority of the population.

Much of the beautifully made work that has survived shows the technical mastery achieved by the craftspeople of ancient times. Everything was handmade and needed a lot of time and effort.

The production of certain materials was concentrated in specific areas. Metalwork, for instance, was done close to mines, and many crafts – such as the manufacture of Attic pottery around Athens and of purple dye in Phoenicia – were carried out where the particular skills originally developed. There was a lively trade, especially in valuable metalwork among the various cultures. This was made possible because the Mediterranean has always been easy to navigate. The name of the island of Cyprus means copper – after the copper that was mined there.

Because their scarcity made them precious, metals were first used for jewellery, statues and weapons, and not for tools.

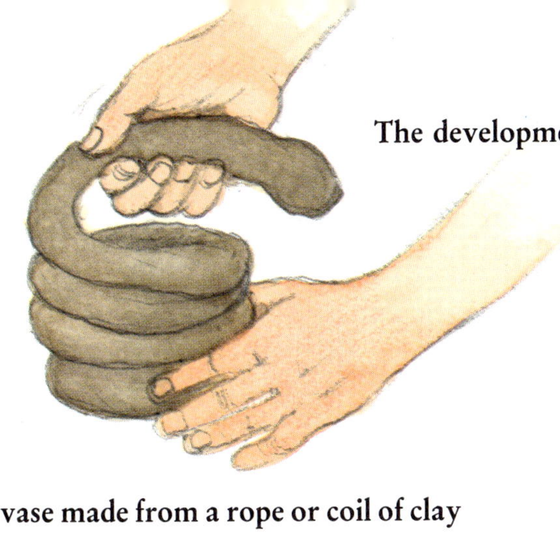

The development of the art of pottery

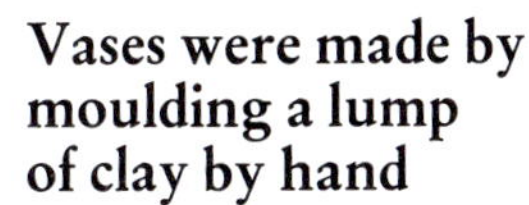

Vases were made by
moulding a lump
of clay by hand

A vase made from a rope or coil of clay

Vases made on two types of turntable. On the left is a simple plate turntable, and on the right two discs joined at the hub by an axle. Both turntables are worked by hand

Primitive skills such as chipping flints and modelling clay led to the first 'machines' which cut down on labour and improved the quality of what was being produced. The potter's wheel, which was originally turned by hand and then by foot in order to leave both hands free, was already in use by 4000 BC. The bow drill was used in ancient Egypt, while Iron Age Europe was already working with the hand-operated lathe around 700 BC.

Syria was midway between the great empires of the Near East and it was the trade crossroads of ancient times. All roads led there, from the Assyro-Babylonian cities, from the Hittite civilization of Asia Minor and from Egypt. Here too, passed the nomadic Bedouin caravans of the Arabian desert.

Crete, a very dry, mountainous island of crowded cities and towns and little agriculture, depended almost entirely on trade for its survival. Like Syria, Crete occupied a central position in the sea-trade, and for many centuries the island controlled sea traffic in the Mediterranean.

The Phoenician cities of Tyre and Sidon along the coast of what is now Lebanon, communicated with each other by sea. Most Phoenicians lived off maritime trade in the Mediterranean.

Trade during those times involved mostly luxury items such as valuable cloth, ointments and perfumes rather than everyday goods. But because transportation was so difficult and expensive, merchants preferred to deal in the least bulky and most valuable goods.

Goods were transported in short stages, no matter how long the journey – the sooner they could be sold, the greater the profit would be. Each area protected its own traders; outsiders were therefore vulnerable to attack and robbery. Markets, which were held outdoors in squares and at gateways, displayed all sorts of exotic items such as ivory and ostrich eggs from Egypt and the gem, lapis lazuli, from Afghanistan.

The slave trade flourished. Slaves were tied and bound, stripped to show their muscles or attractiveness and exhibited in public squares.

As trade flourished, writing became essential. Writing evolved from the need to record warehouse stocks and the movements of goods and do accounts.

A vase (*ekythos*)

An amphora (*a two-handled vessel*)

A pitcher (*oinokoe*)

17

In ancient times, fashions in clothing changed slowly. Good taste and elegance were cultivated under the pharaohs of Egypt but fashions did not change at all. Ancient Egyptian jewellery and accessories of gold and precious stones show how extravagantly some people dressed. The style of bracelets, necklaces, earrings, hair ornaments, head-dresses, belts and even make-up indicated the class of the aristocracy or civil service to which a person belonged. Egyptian women usually wore clothes made of the finest linen. Wool was considered impure and never used, perhaps because it was not needed in such a warm climate.

Although Cretan women followed Egyptian fashions, Greek women before the classical period dressed in the *chiton*. This long tunic of light wool was elegantly draped and often weighted with lead at the hem so that it would hang gracefully. Some Greek women lightened their hair with a solution called lye or with herbs, but most just plaited their hair. They wore little make-up and used only light perfumes. Much later Greek women began to wear fine cloth of bright colours, footwear with high heels, necklaces and scented ornaments. In fact, the *peplos* – a shawl-like garment worn by women – became so ornate that certain philsophers expressed disapproval, although many men dressed just as elaborately.

Greek clothes

The chiton

**The *himaton*
(a cloak)**

**The chiton
worn by men**

*The **chiton** worn by Greek men was a single, long rectangle of cloth wound around the body and folded back over one shoulder. The men wore leather sandals and usually went bare-headed. However, they did wear broad-brimmed hats for travel or special occasions.*
*Each year Athenian girls wove a special **peplos** which they carried in a ritual procession to the temple of the goddess Athena as a gift on her feast day.*

Egyptian clothes

A sandal – worn by all social classes

The nemeth, the Egyptian man's head-dress

Typical plaited hairstyle adorned with jewels

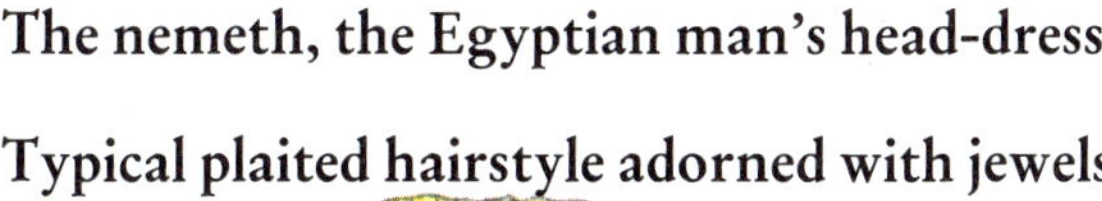

Egyptian men wore a simple knee-length loincloth made of fine linen for the rich, and animal hide or coarse woven fibre for the poor. Egyptian dignitaries never appeared in public with bare heads, and although the normal headgear was a cloth which hung down to the shoulders, all kinds of wigs and symbolic head-dresses were also worn.

19

The simplest and oldest forms of transport was riding on the backs of animals and being pulled on a sledge behind an animal. Heavy weights, such as the blocks of stone used in the Egyptian pyramids, were moved for centuries by means of wooden rollers – the ancestors of the wheel. The first wheeled carts were the funeral carriages pulled by wild donkeys in about 3000 BC in Mesopotamia. It is believed that the Scythians of the Asian steppes domesticated horses to pull the carts at a later date.

Transport by water was easier than on land. Rafts were floated on hide sacks pumped full of air, while boats made of animal hides, but with wooden decks, sailed the rivers of Mesopotamia. On the calm waters of the Nile, the Egyptians used boats made of bundles of papyrus. For sea travel vessels were made of wood.

The greatest sailors in ancient times were the Phoenicians, who established trading centres all over the Mediterranean. They founded colonies in northern Africa, Sicily, Sardinia and Spain. Little is known about Phoenician ships except that they first used anchors in about 1000 BC. Phoenician coins have been found as far from the Mediterranean as the Azores, in the Atlantic Ocean.

An essential feature of the Greek *galley* was the keel. This stabilized the boat lengthwise and so allowed the Greeks to cross the open sea rather than hug the coast. Merchant galleys had a single mast with a square sail. War galleys always had a miniature castle at the prow, and two, or sometimes three tiers of oarsmen.

The Persians built a royal road across their entire empire, from Sardis in Asia Minor, close to the Aegean shore, to Susa, beyond Babylon. The best means of travel was by horse, although mules and camels were also used. Like the Egyptians, the Persians had an efficient postal service, with posting stations located about every 25 kilometres. This meant that a hard-riding messenger could cover up to 150 kilometres a day.

A Greek galley

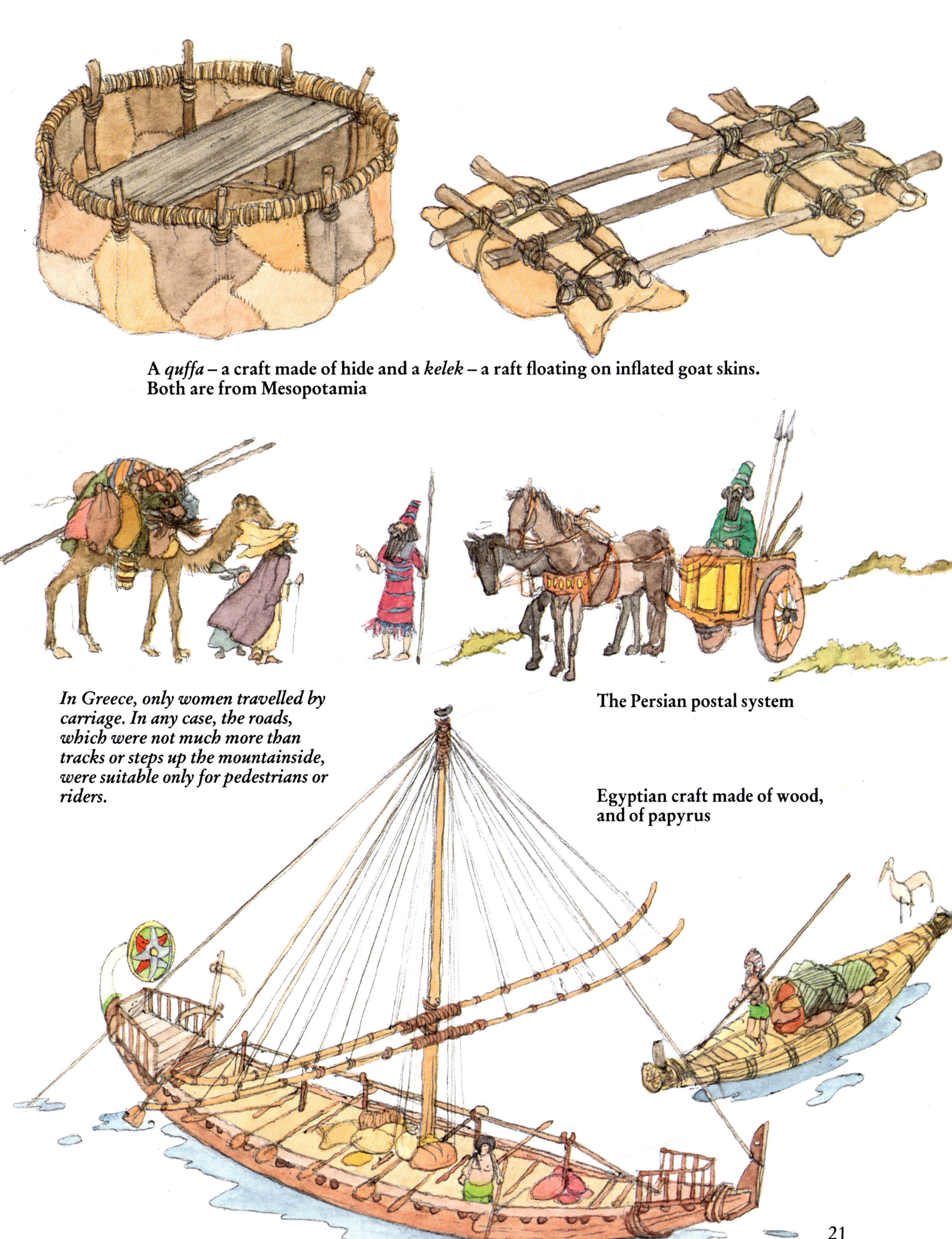

A *quffa* – a craft made of hide and a *kelek* – a raft floating on inflated goat skins.
Both are from Mesopotamia

In Greece, only women travelled by carriage. In any case, the roads, which were not much more than tracks or steps up the mountainside, were suitable only for pedestrians or riders.

The Persian postal system

Egyptian craft made of wood, and of papyrus

The primitive life of the Stone Age did not change until metal came into use for making stronger and more durable tools. The extraction and melting down of metals was one of the greatest discoveries of the past. For this reason, the various periods of prehistory are named the Copper, Bronze and Iron Ages. It is still not known how early people achieved the high temperatures necessary for melting metal, or how they were able to produce such delicate craftsmanship.

In addition to metalwork, several other key discoveries helped to stimulate the progress of Western civilization. In the mines, rock was shattered by means of sudden, extreme changes in temperature. First the rock was heated with fire and then cold water was poured over it. This use of fire and water was one of the earliest technological breakthroughs. The arch, which can be seen in much Roman architecture, was an important invention. The wheel was originally a solid circle of wood, made lighter for war chariots by means of hoops and spokes. Simple tools such as the lever, the pulley, the compass and locking devices that used keys, made an enormous difference to everyday life.

Writing is one of the most important inventions of all time. In 4000 BC, the Sumerians already had a system of pictograms (picture symbols). This evolved into a kind of writing known as *cuneiform*. This involved scratching wedge-shaped letters on to wet clay tablets with a sharp tool. The tablet was then baked to preserve the writing. The entire Sumerian language was represented by just seven wedge shapes used in different combinations.

Egyptian *hieroglyphic* writing hardly changed over thousands of years. Although it might seem that each symbol represented the corresponding object, it actually represented a sound. Because there were no symbols for vowel sounds, additional figures were often inserted to make the meaning clearer.

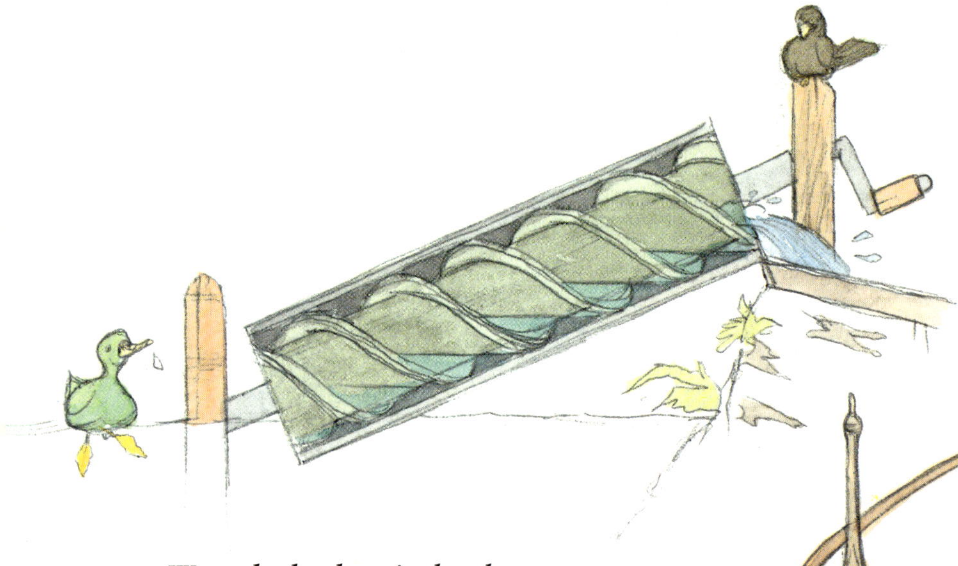

Fire was started by rubbing wood against wood. A stick of wood was spun at great speed in the hollow of another piece of wood.

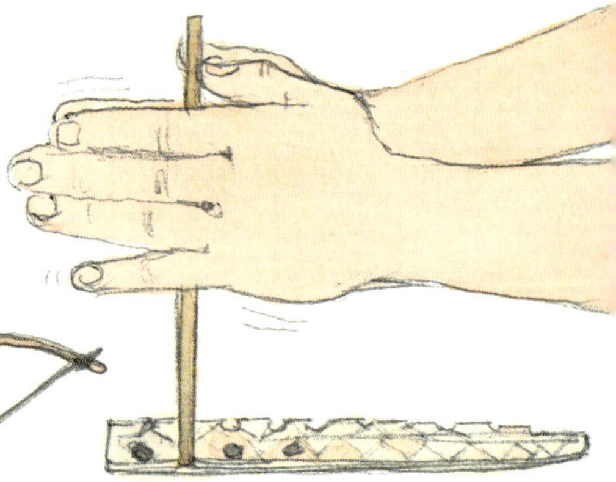

Water had to be raised and channelled to irrigate the fields. 'Archimedes screw' (cochlea) was the earliest form of pump.

As soon as it started smoking, it was touched against straw or dry leaves to ignite a fire.

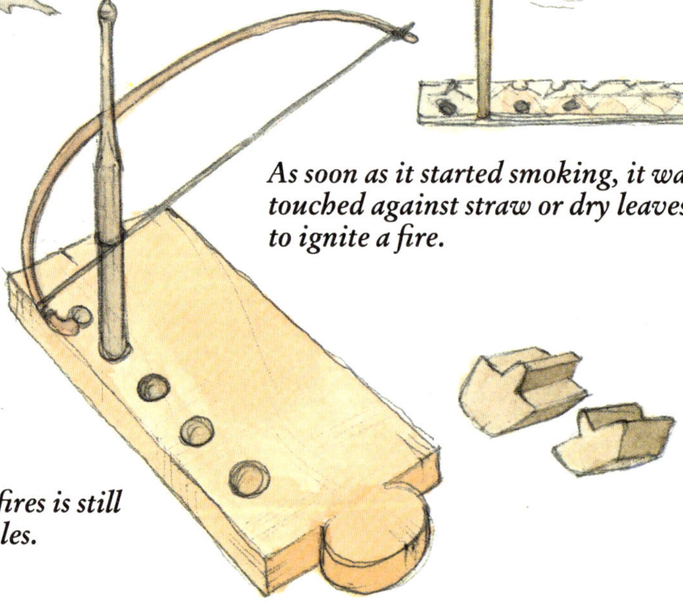

This method of lighting fires is still used today by some peoples.

The Greek mathematician and inventor, Hero, noticed how gas expands when heated and thought of turning heat into mechanical energy. At the time his theory was only used to open and close temple doors automatically, but the principle would later be applied to create engines, like the one that moves a car.

Egyptian hieroglyphics, other than those on papyrus, appeared on mural inscriptions or sculptured in stone. Certain masons specialized in this type of decoration.

The evolution of cuneiform writing

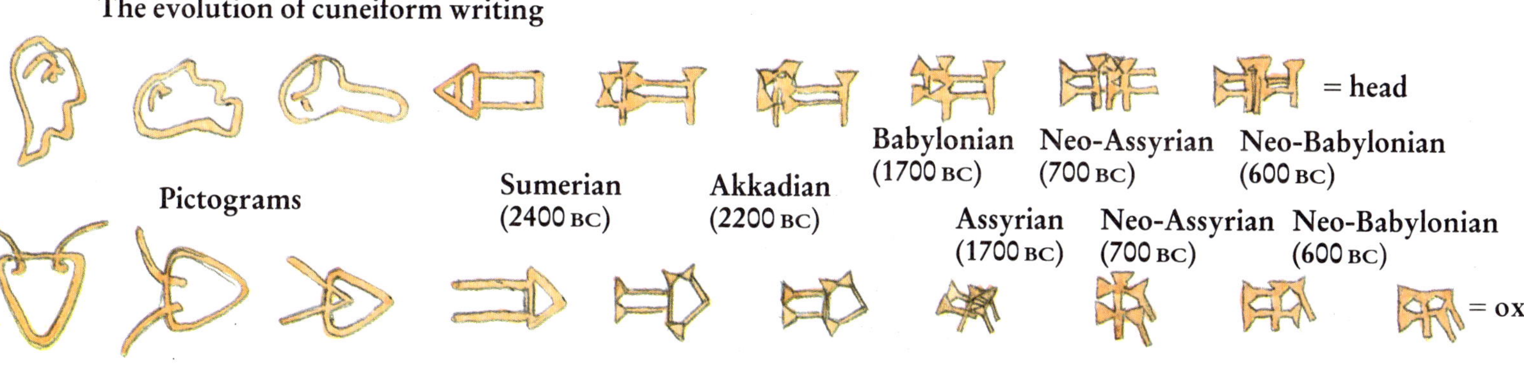

Most of the soldiers who fought for the great empires were slaves. They were trained to use weapons and kept physically fit so that they could endure the long marches and hardships of war. Battles were won by carefully planned tactics as well as by physical strength. The cream of the aristocracy directed the armies, with the most important campaigns being led by the ruler himself, accompanied by his war council.

In 2000 BC, Hittites, Egyptians, Assyrians and Babylonians fought constantly for control of the trade crossroads in Syria. The crossroads were also the route used by invaders from the Asian steppes. With the rise of other western powers, first in Greece and then in Italy, the conflict between East and West began.

In the Greek city-state, the regular soldier was the free man who could supply his own armour and weapons, called *panoplia*. In Sparta, which was a military state, soldiers lived in barracks until they were thirty, when they were allowed to marry. Married or not, they continued their military service until they were sixty.

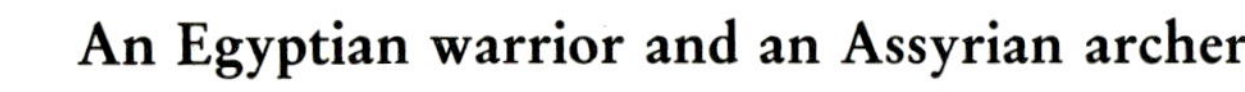

An Egyptian warrior and an Assyrian archer

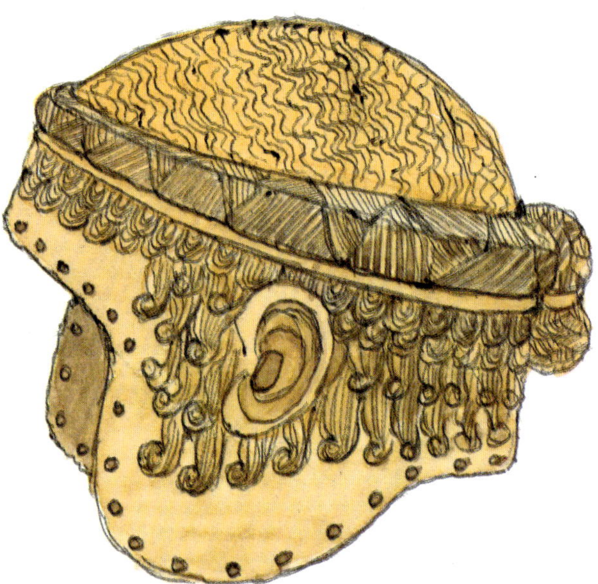

The bronze helmet of Sargon, the first ruler to create a vast empire in Mesopotamia.

The most famous family of heroes was the Acheians, who destroyed Troy in about 1250 BC. Achilles, Diomedes, Ajax and Ulysses, as well as the Trojans, Hector and Aeneas, live on in the great epic stories of Homer.

Arranging soldiers in phalanxes dates back at least to
Egyptian times. In a phalanx, shields were held side by side,
forming a protective wall, while spears were thrust forward.
This formation helped to repulse the enemy. The first attack,
using bows and arrows and slings was made from a distance.
The cavalry then came in to break up the enemy lines so that
the infantry could engage in hand-to-hand combat.

A Macedonian warrior
carrying a long lance

In the middle of the second
millennium BC, war chariots appeared
in all great empires, built on more or
less the same model. Their speed and
strength made them terrifying. The
charioteer held the horses and kept the
chariot on an even course, so allowing
the soldier behind him to throw
javelins and shoot arrows.

Imperial Rome

Rome began as a small republic, no different from the earlier Etruscan city-states and Greek colonies. Its head magistrates were two consuls elected by the *senate*, a body of men representing the *patrician*, or aristocratic, class. The *plebeians*, or common people, had their own magistrates, known as *tribunes*.

After Rome conquered all the lands that bordered the Mediterranean, civil war broke out between the leading officers of the army. As a result, power came to rest in the hands of one person, the emperor, who held his position for life.

The Roman Empire was at its greatest size around AD 100, when it stretched from Britain

Roman women played an important role in court intrigues and palace plots. Some were educated, but for the most part the 'ideal woman' was a faithful wife and devoted mother who ran her huge household efficiently.

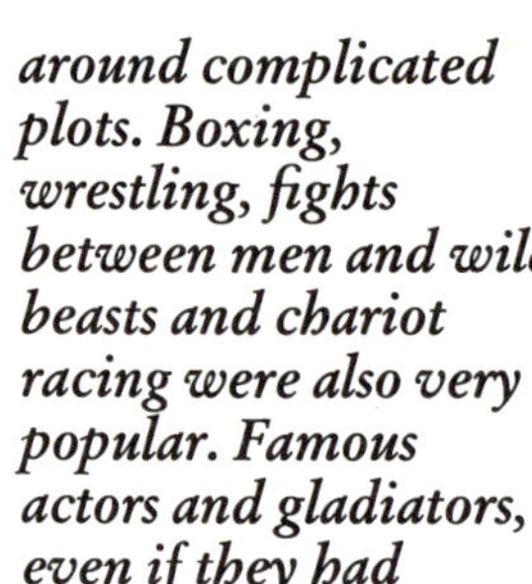
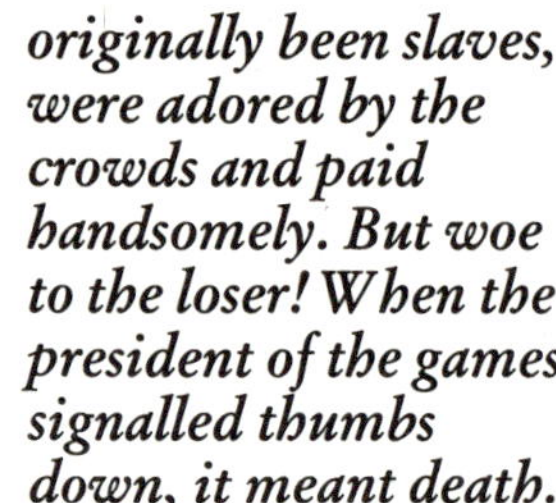

Although poets and artists were greatly honoured and often enjoyed special privileges, the Romans loved the theatre, and above all the circus. Plays, and especially comedies, revolved around complicated plots. Boxing, wrestling, fights between men and wild beasts and chariot racing were also very popular. Famous actors and gladiators, even if they had originally been slaves, were adored by the crowds and paid handsomely. But woe to the loser! When the president of the games signalled thumbs down, it meant death.

to Africa and from Spain to Syria. At this time the Emperor Hadrian decided to concentrate on ruling his vast empire rather than making more conquests. In reaching decisions, the Emperor consulted the senate, which still represented the upper aristocracy and had retained at least some of its former power.

The Romans believed that power was not given by the gods, but was based on military strength and by popular support. Roman citizenship was gradually extended to all free men in the Empire. Even slaves could become free citizens (*liberti*), either through the generosity of their owners or by paying a large ransom. Nevertheless, the great majority of the poor, as well as conquered subjects of other states, remained slaves. They were still forced to work in the fields under masters who held the power of life and death over them. Not surprisingly, the slaves revolted from time to time. One of the most famous revolts was led by Spartacus. The penalty for such action was to be nailed to a tree, covered with pitch and burned to death.

Like soldiers and magistrates, patricians were for the most part landowners, while the slaves, apart from those who were miners, craftsmen, or galley oarsmen, worked in the fields. The wealth of the Empire depended on its agriculture.

27

The typical Roman patrician's house, whether in town or in the country, was a villa. It was large and built around a square courtyard with *porticoes* and balconies. In it lived the household slaves as well as the family.

In the country villa, there were storehouses for carts and tools. If the *pater familias* (the male head of the household) was a tradesman, the town villa would have shops and workshops on the ground floor, with living space on top (see illustration below). If the owner was a financier, politician, soldier, professional or literary man, the villa had grand suites of rooms. Public quarters were for outsiders who came and went, while private quarters for the family included bedrooms, a kitchen, a pantry, service rooms and a *triclinium*, where meals were eaten while reclining on couches.

Ordinary townspeople lived in *insulae* – huge residential blocks, several floors high which were bounded on all four sides by streets. The ground floor was lined with shops and workshops which often spilled out into the teeming, bustling streets. The magistrates who were in charge of housing and water made sure that the residences were clean and well maintained. With its eleven aqueducts, Rome probably had the best water supply of any ancient city and in about AD 400, it could also boast a good sewage system and 144 public lavatories.

Cities and towns founded or redesigned by the Romans usually followed an orderly plan of straight streets laid out at right-angles to each other around a focal point. The central square, or *forum*, with its temple and *basilica*, was located where the two main streets met.

The one-family house of the artisan, tradesman or small independent farmer remained virtually unchanged for centuries. There was a workshop or shop, and barn or shed for equipment downstairs.

Upstairs, there was a bedroom and a living-room. Both water and fire were kept outside the living area. Heat was provided by a small oven inside the house. Braziers and oil lamps were used for lighting.

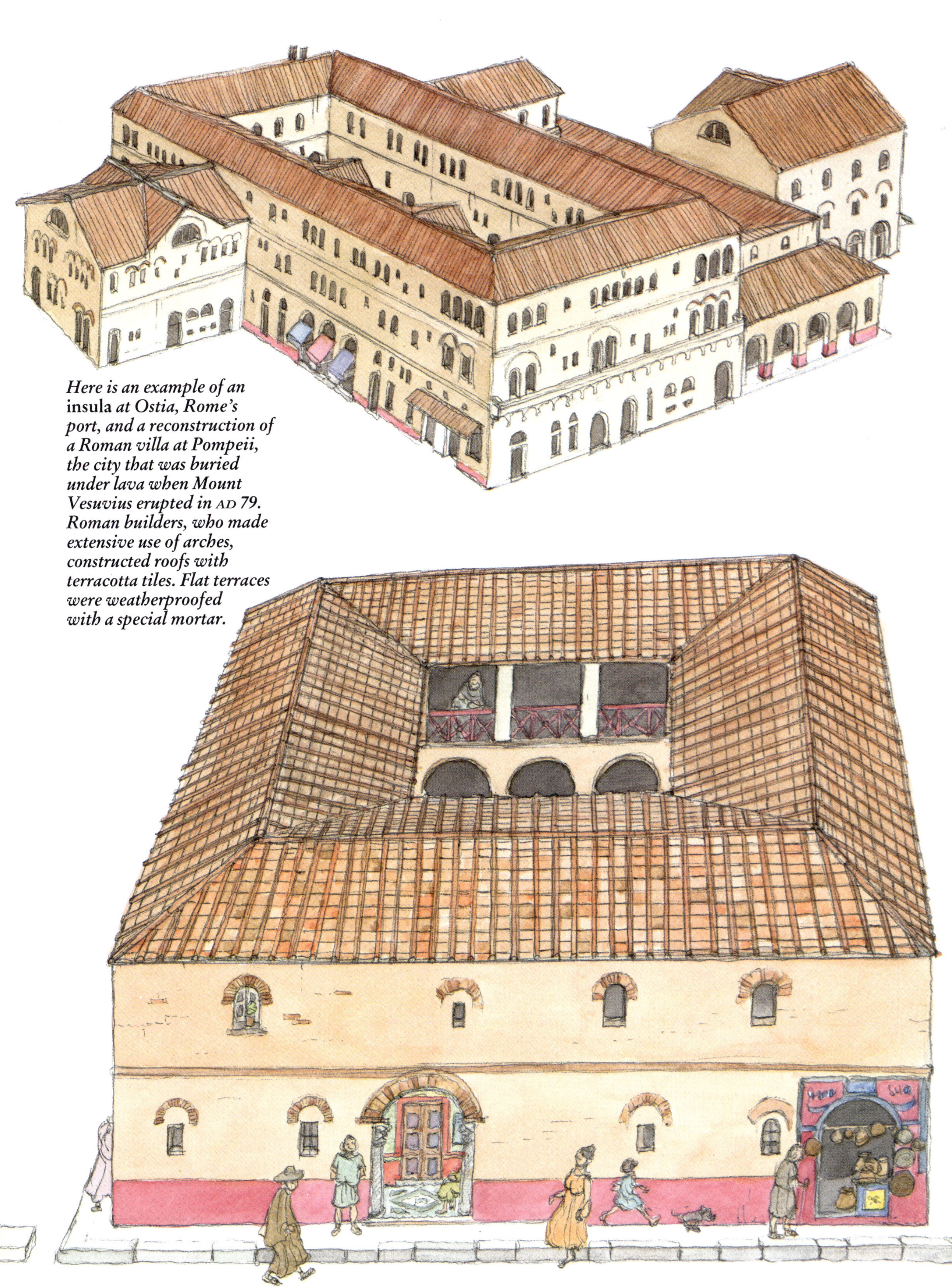

Here is an example of an insula *at Ostia, Rome's port, and a reconstruction of a Roman villa at Pompeii, the city that was buried under lava when Mount Vesuvius erupted in AD 79. Roman builders, who made extensive use of arches, constructed roofs with terracotta tiles. Flat terraces were weatherproofed with a special mortar.*

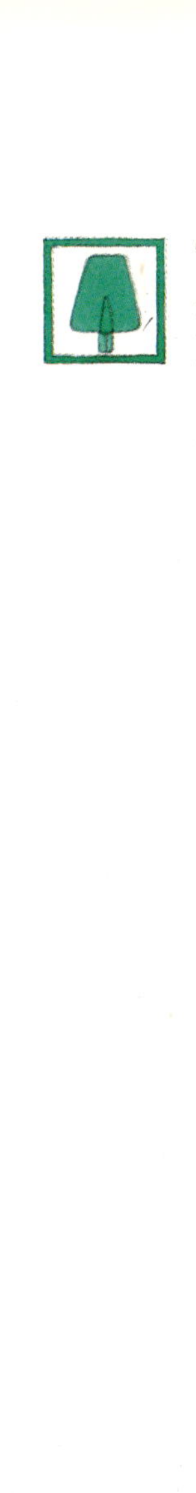 There were two types of Roman farms – the family business run by the *pater familias* and his wife, children and servants, and the large estate worked by slaves. With little manpower, the small farmer had no time for studying or trying out new tools that might have increased his productivity and lightened his work. His aim was not to sell vast quantities of produce, but simply to support his family and make them as comfortable as possible. He raised crops that varied from cereals to vegetables and fruit, and cultivated grapevines for wine, olive trees for olive oil and woodland for timber.

When they retired from active service, soldiers of the Empire were given farmland. When possible, they chose the most fertile areas that had either springs or rivers available for irrigation. Great stretches of marshland were also reclaimed, among them the Po Valley in Italy, the mouth of the Rhône River in southern France, and the land around modern Cambridge in England. This reclamation not only made more land available for farming, but also reduced diseases such as malaria.

Careful management was needed to farm the land. For instance, farming land had to be carefully divided amongst labourers. The Romans were expert at dividing the land evenly into suitable farm sizes. They used an instrument called a **groma** *to mark out the right-angled corners of farmland. Because the soil was double-ploughed crosswise, the fields were square.*

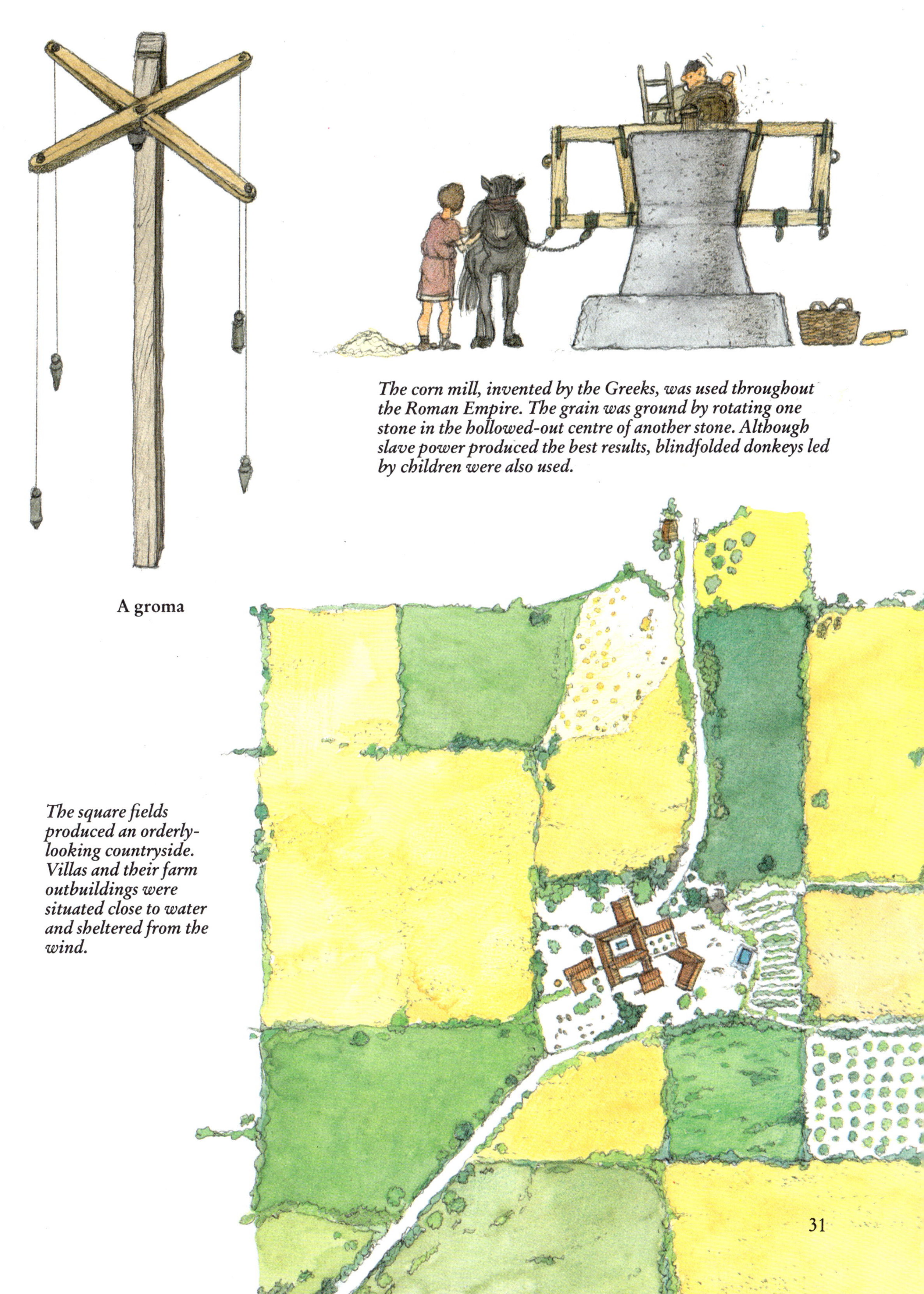

A groma

The corn mill, invented by the Greeks, was used throughout the Roman Empire. The grain was ground by rotating one stone in the hollowed-out centre of another stone. Although slave power produced the best results, blindfolded donkeys led by children were also used.

The square fields produced an orderly-looking countryside. Villas and their farm outbuildings were situated close to water and sheltered from the wind.

The Romans' huge building programmes required many skilled architects and craftsmen. As a building grew higher, stone blocks were raised up inclines that were built higher and higher until the building was finished and the inclines could be removed. Teams of men with strong ropes hoisted columns and obelisks into place. Precise calculations guaranteed that each piece would be moved into exactly the right position. Sometimes pulleys were attached to a wheel turned by men walking inside it.

Using the same principle with water power, the Romans invented the water mill, which enabled flour to be produced on a large scale. The mills were mainly in the centre of the Empire with the old manually powered mil's being used elsewhere. The mill and oven were often in the same building. This meant that grain would go in and bread would come out.

In a city like Rome, with over a million inhabitants, there was a thriving clothing trade. At times of crisis, the *plebeians* (common people), rather than trying to increase their production, simply demanded free handouts of corn. To avoid trouble, such requests were usually granted. Many goods were imported from the provinces. The East was the best source of luxury items such as fine woven and dyed materials, jewellery and perfume. The Romans always admired the Greeks for their artistic traditions, and in the second century BC, the Emperor Hadrian summoned all the best Greek artists to come to Rome to revive Greek styles. Egyptian obelisks were brought to Rome to make the city more attractive. In fact most of the ancient obelisks that have survived to this day are found in Rome.

Many people worked to turn farm produce into food. The basic food was a sort of wholemeal bread made with unprocessed flour, which was rather acidic because of the enzymes used to make it rise.

Roman streets were crammed with people as well as small shops and workshops. Blacksmiths, coppersmiths, weavers, carders, tanners and cobblers, as well as people transporting materials, set up their benches in the thoroughfares. The city was filled with the hammering of anvils and the sawing of wood; with bustle, smoke, noise and smells – some delicious and some not so delicious!

At the height of the Empire, the city of Rome alone consumed virtually all the produce paid as tribute by Sicily, Egypt and the African provinces, as well as huge quantites of grain and oil which were imported by private merchants from Spain.

The large cities served as both administrative centres and trading posts for goods travelling to and from Rome along the Empire's vast network of roads and waterways. Even in the most distant provinces, people tried to copy the Roman life-style. Creating the means to transport goods quickly was essential in this world of intense trade between different regions. Transporting goods became easier with minimal customs barriers, a single currency, well-maintained roads and ports and an almost total absence of piracy.

Nevertheless, Rome, with its free market and thousands of small traders, never introduced a unified trading system on which it could concentrate its resources. Goods were distributed through small-scale outlets, with dealers specializing in just one type of product. This meant that merchandise, such as incense and wild beasts from Ethiopia (for use in the circuses), spices from India and silk from China, often travelled hundreds of kilometres and passed through many hands only to end up in some tiny shop in Rome.

The main Mediterranean port was Alexandria in northern Africa, with a population of half a million. The great caravan routes, protected by border towns such as Palmyra and Petra, led eastward from the Syrian coastal ports, and from Antioch to Gaza. Greek, Phoenician and Arabian merchants had to ask permission from Rome to travel around the Mediterranean and down the Red Sea into the Persian Gulf.

Apart from grain crises in Roman colonies in Greece, the provinces were self-sufficient in food and everyday goods. Trade involved mainly luxury items such as fine pottery, skilfully worked glass, jewellery, ointments, cloth, carpets and works of art. Papyrus was used throughout the Mediterranean world for writing.

Tonsor, the barber

Lanius, the butcher

Vinarius, the wineshop keeper

Pomarius, the greengrocer

A Roman coin showing the head of a goddess. Coins had the ruler's head on one side as coins do today.

Taberna, the inn

The finest of the world's goods could be found in Rome, where distribution was handled through a network of specialized shops.

 The *tunic*, originally sleeveless, was a basic Roman garment worn only by Roman citizens after they had come of age. For warmth, some men, such as the Emperor Augustus, wore more than one. The tunic, which was pulled on over the head, was normally knee-length, although later it was worn ankle-length. Men only wore belts outdoors. The *toga* was a garment which was pulled on over the tunic and wrapped around the body. Different types of toga showed the wearer's social position or rank. Priests and magistrates wore a *toga praetexta* with a purple band in front while the all-white *toga candida*, worn without a tunic to display war wounds, identified candidates for the civil service and public positions.

There were various styles of sandals: some laced around the feet while others strapped up the calf of the leg. Women's footwear included the *soccus*, a comfortable slipper. Over their tunic which tied at the sides and under the breasts, women wore a *palla*. This was a wide mantle which passed under the right arm and hung over the left shoulder to the ground. Jewelled gold brooches kept clothes and hair in place. Rings glittered on the fingers and engaged couples exchanged gold-plated iron rings that were worn on the left-hand ring finger. The Romans believed that this finger was connected by a nerve to the heart.

Like the Greeks, the Romans wore hats only for travelling. When young men donned the adult toga, they kept their arms covered up for a year as a token of humility.

Lacerna, a heavy cloak

Women's fashions changed frequently and Roman women, who loved fine materials, bright colours, and rich embroidery, wore elaborate clothing.

Carbatina, a popular sandal

The earliest Romans were mostly shepherds living in the hills of Latium and they knew little about the sea. It is believed that a Carthaginian ship that was wrecked on the shores of Italy was the original model for Roman ships. Eventually, the Romans used the most sophisticated technology of the period to build a navy that was unsurpassed for over a thousand years.

Once the Mediterranean was conquered and purged of pirates, a merchant fleet was built to bring goods to Rome from the provinces. In order to increase safety, especially in storms, these trading vessels – *onorariae* – were redesigned and improved. They differed from fighting ships. The hull was more solid and curved and the stern was taller and broader to allow for a larger sail. The massive main mast consisted of several shafts lashed tightly together, while a foresail ensured manoeuvrability at the bow. Two additional triangular topsails were hoisted above the square sail, between the mast and the two yardarms. Many ships had deck cabins for the sailors, and a gallery on the poop deck held a shrine to the patron god.

The Roman road system was well developed. From about AD 100 to 150, the road network stretched uninterrupted, except for the sea, from Hadrian's Wall in northern *Britannia* (Roman Britain) to the edge of the Sahara, and from the Straits of Gibraltar to the Persian Gulf. These roads were built and paved in three layers. A foundation of stone blocks was covered with packed rubble which in turn was hardened with mortar. All of this was topped with paving stones. Europe did not see a road network of such quality for another thousand years or more. Of special importance were the passes over the Alps which, ironically, were used by the invaders who eventually conquered Rome.

Roman warships were built for attack rather than for strategic manoeuvres. Enemy warships were rammed and then boarded across a special gangway bridge which was thrown out from the Roman ship's bow. This bridge was dropped down on to the enemy ship to link the two vessels together.

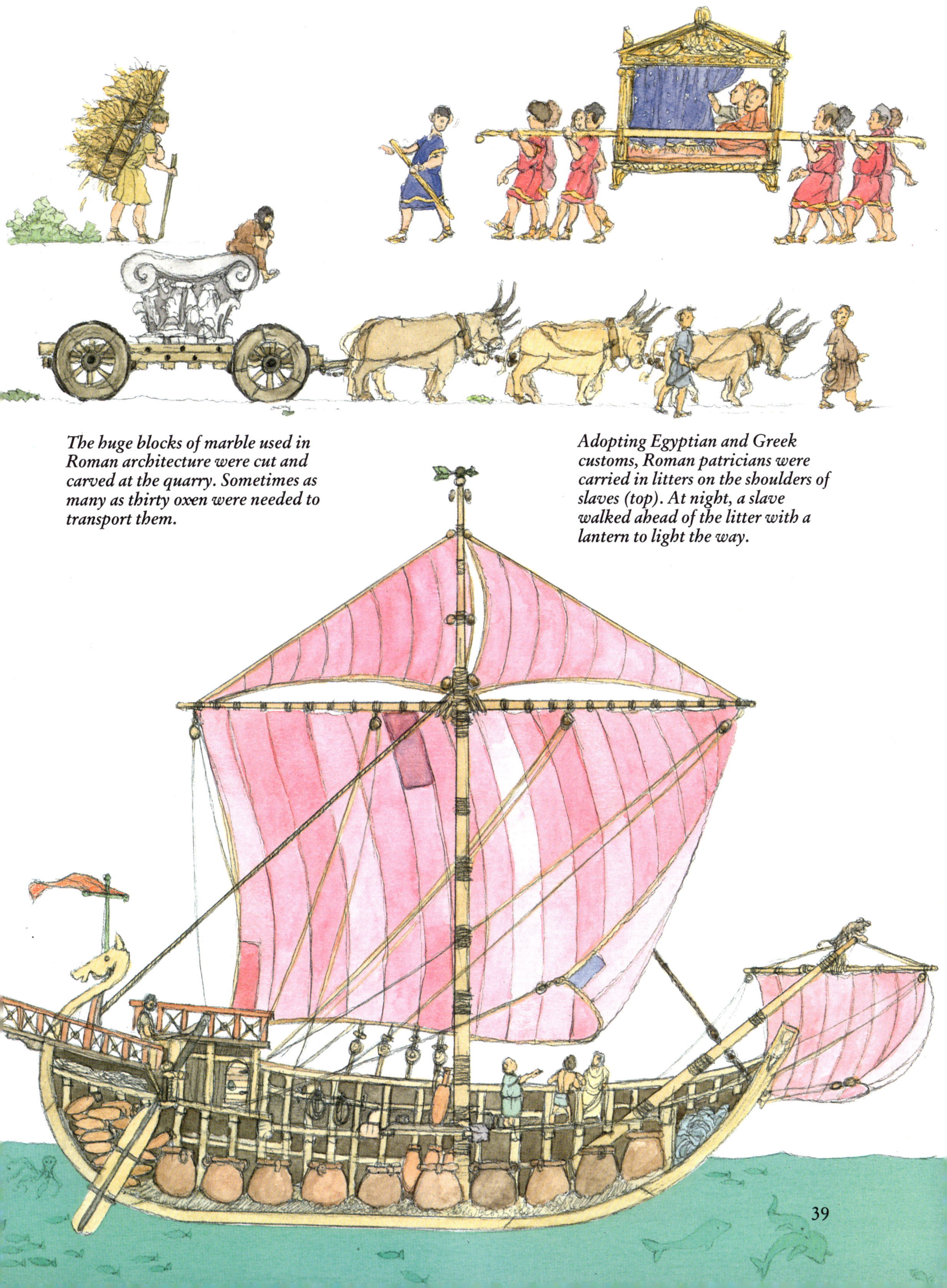

The huge blocks of marble used in Roman architecture were cut and carved at the quarry. Sometimes as many as thirty oxen were needed to transport them.

Adopting Egyptian and Greek customs, Roman patricians were carried in litters on the shoulders of slaves (top). At night, a slave walked ahead of the litter with a lantern to light the way.

The clearest evidence today of Roman occupation of an area can be seen in the buildings which were left behind. As builders, the Romans surpassed all earlier civilizations. They established three basic laws of architecture: *firmitas*, (solidity); *utilitas*, (the purpose of any particular building) and *venustas*, (order and beauty). Arches, which had been used experimentally by the Etruscans, were developed and perfected so that it was possible to have large empty spaces between supporting pillars without the need for wooden beams or stone lintels. Wood was perishable and both wood and stone were bulky, awkward to position and fragile under heavy loads. Light, elegant buildings with galleries of arches were not only easy to build because they were constructed with small stones or bricks, but also economical because they required less load-bearing structure.

The Romans were the first to use water for mechanical power. Power was harnessed by using rivers to turn paddle wheels connected to shafts. The result? The original water mill.

Adequate drinking water was a constant source of concern for Roman administrators. The solution was to supply water from wells or springs, sometimes many kilometres from the city, along aqueducts. Aqueducts consisted of channels, lead piping and syphons supported by bridges of slender, tiered arcades. In about AD 100, Rome had nine aqueducts. Later, this number grew to as many as nineteen.

Although the Roman Empire was always interested in finding new lands to conquer, the huge size of the Empire, combined with its almost unlimited supply of low-cost labour, meant that there was little incentive to find new resources or advance technology. This was certainly not the case for either the government or the army, the two spheres of influence in which Roman genius showed itself most fully. All later Western legal systems have been based on Roman law.

In Rome, water was distributed along small pipes. In about AD 200, there were 11 public baths and over 800 private ones, while 1300 public fountains and cisterns provided hundreds of litres of water every day for each person.

Patrician villas developed a hot-water heating system, complete with an outside boiler to heat the water, which then flowed under the floors, warming them. Even ships had plumbing systems.

An aqueduct under construction

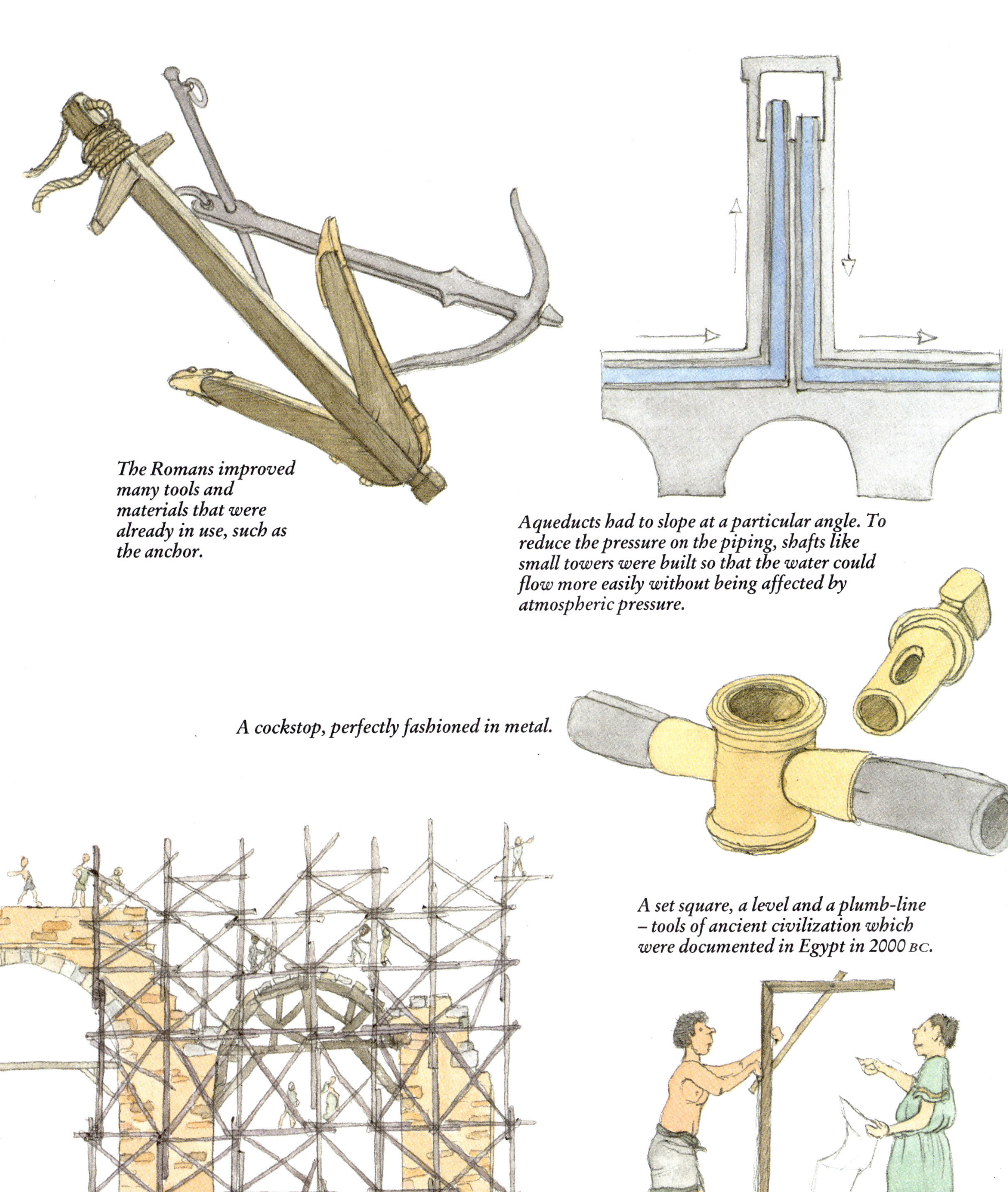

The Romans improved many tools and materials that were already in use, such as the anchor.

Aqueducts had to slope at a particular angle. To reduce the pressure on the piping, shafts like small towers were built so that the water could flow more easily without being affected by atmospheric pressure.

A cockstop, perfectly fashioned in metal.

A set square, a level and a plumb-line – tools of ancient civilization which were documented in Egypt in 2000 BC.

Under the Roman Republic, the army was made up of those free citizens who could afford to equip and arm themselves and who had interests and land to defend.

Any male Roman citizen, no matter how poor he was or where he came from, could enter the *legions*. Armed and supported by the state, these soldiers, who were loyal to their generals as well as to Rome, threw themselves into adventure and conquest. At the same time they added to their own personal prestige. Rivalry between generals attempting to seize power in Rome caused bloody civil wars. After the death of Julius Caesar – the true founder of the Empire although he never took the title of emperor – many successful war-lords were hailed as emperor by their legions and were kept on the throne by their armies.

The Roman army was able to conquer such a vast empire because of its fine equipment and training, its perfectly organized ranks and, above all, its strict discipline.

A Gaul and a German

A standard bearer

A legionary with his kit

Left: The distinction between light and heavy infantry disappeared as all soldiers began to carry a sword and spear. The spears were designed to break after they were thrown so that they could not be used by the enemy. Rectangular shields replaced oval ones in the first century BC.

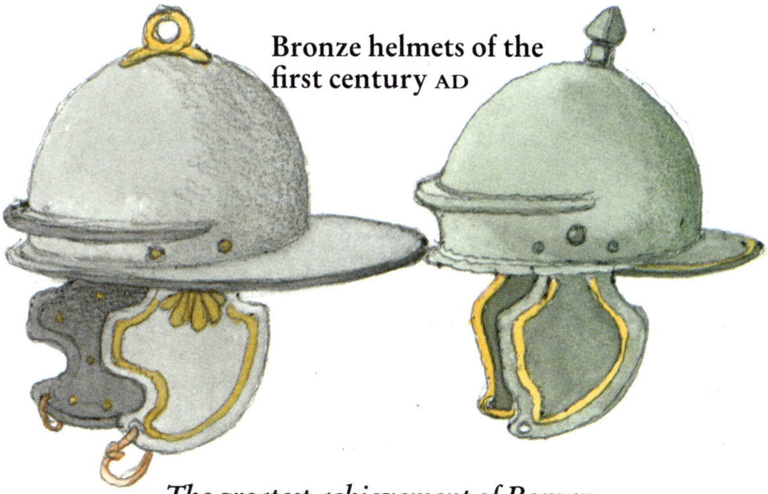

Bronze helmets of the first century AD

The greatest achievement of Roman military engineering was the building of a bridge over the Rhine River in just ten days and the dismantling of it two weeks later. Siege machines featured rams for battering down walls and doors, catapults for hurling missiles and flaming torches, and bridges with hooks for clamping on to enemy forts.

A military square formation

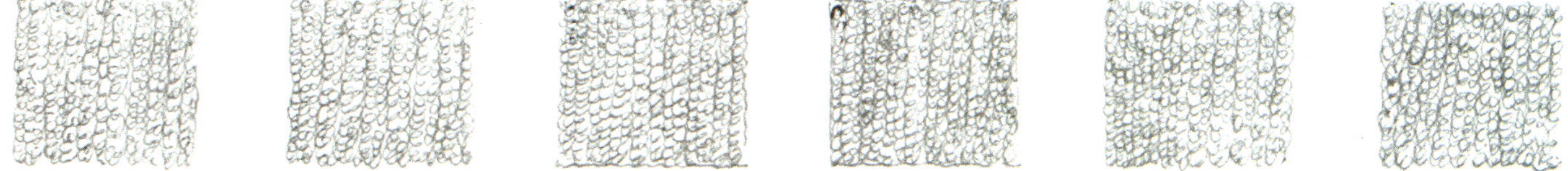

Squads of 120 men, maniples – were drawn up in several ranks, with soldiers staggered in alternating lines. This meant they could 'close ranks' on all four sides. If the enemy managed to split the formation, the soldiers could still defend themselves in compact squares. In extreme cases, or if they were set upon in open country, a group of men formed a 'tortoise' formation, using their shields to cover their sides and heads. This enabled them to withstand even a chariot attack.

# The First Millennium

Emperor

Although the Romans had set up well-fortified lines of defence along the Rhine and Danube, hordes of Huns from the eastern European steppes invaded from the north, changing the political map of the Western Roman Empire within a matter of decades. These primitive, war-like tribes swept across Europe in their thirst for conquest.

After the Roman legions were gone, the struggle for power and a reorganized empire continued among different groups of invaders under their various leaders and kings. First the Franks, then the Saxons and later the Swabians sought control of the empire. It was now called the Holy Roman Empire because it had become recognized by the Church and its emperors were crowned by the Pope.

The new system of social organization, called *feudalism*, was based on the *fief*, or feud – an area administered by a feudal lord

Feudal lords

Pope

High clergy

Knights

The military class retained its importance. The imperial army had to keep the Empire together, even when this meant using force internally. The army also had to stop the hordes of Vikings in the north, Magyars in the east and Saracens in the south.

Clerics

Two major groups enjoyed certain freedoms: craftsmen, who began to organize themselves into companies and guilds, and the top officials of the Church hierarchy, who for a long time represented society's only stable authority. The large numbers of farm labourers, the glebe serfs, were the lowest of the feudal social order.

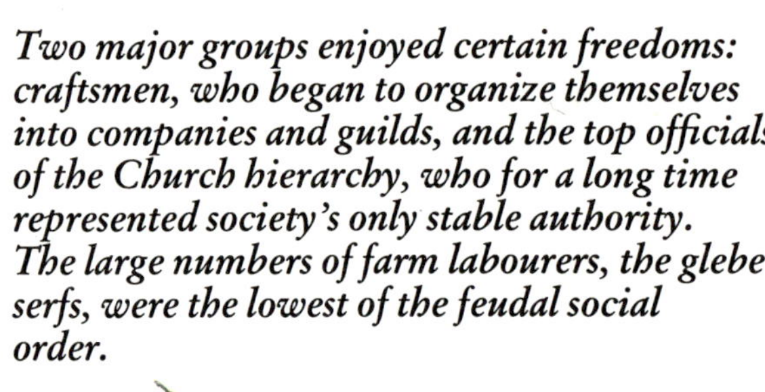

Artisans

Servants

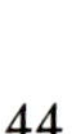

appointed by the emperor. This feudal lord, in turn, had others under him, right down to the lowest *vassal*. Once fiefs became hereditary, a new aristocracy was born and a nobility emerged. The centre of the feud was the lord's castle. Peasant villages clustered around it so that when danger threatened, the peasants could flee inside the castle and defend it.

Devastation and plague resulted in a famine, which led to a sharp drop in population. Eventually everyone, whatever their social position, had to help rebuild society. The Christian Church, which was now spreading throughout the West, acted as a moral spur. The Benedictines contributed greatly by setting an example to the rest of the community.

The abbot, who was often a bishop, was elected by the monks to be in charge of the monastery. Each monk had his own tasks of work and prayer. The scribes, or amanuenses, *had the vital job of copying the works of both classical authors and the Church fathers. This brought together the cultural heritage of the Romans and the new culture of medieval Christendom from which the universities emerged.*

The Abbot

Members of the chapter

Scribes

The various activities of the monastery

The people of northern Europe, some of whom were still semi-nomadic and unfamiliar with city life, developed their own types of dwellings that usually housed more than one family. Living in a cold climate meant that fire, essential for survival, was the focal point of the house. Sloping roofs allowed rain and melted snow to drain off, while smoke from the fire escaped through a small hole at the top of the roof where the support poles met.

Building techniques called half-timbering, based on a wooden framework, were popular for centuries, partly because trees were so plentiful.

Villages, normally built around a central spring or well, were surrounded by a protective ditch which was often reinforced by a sturdy fence or *palisade*. In addition to people's houses, there were also enclosures for animals. The most important of these were horses, used for work and transport, and pigs, which provided meat for the winter. Although the nobles' castles had a similar layout, the walls and towers rested on solid stone foundations, while the roofs might be covered with metal sheets.

The towns founded by the Romans were abandoned and left in ruins after the barbarian invasions. The new centres of growth became the feudal castles and the monasteries.

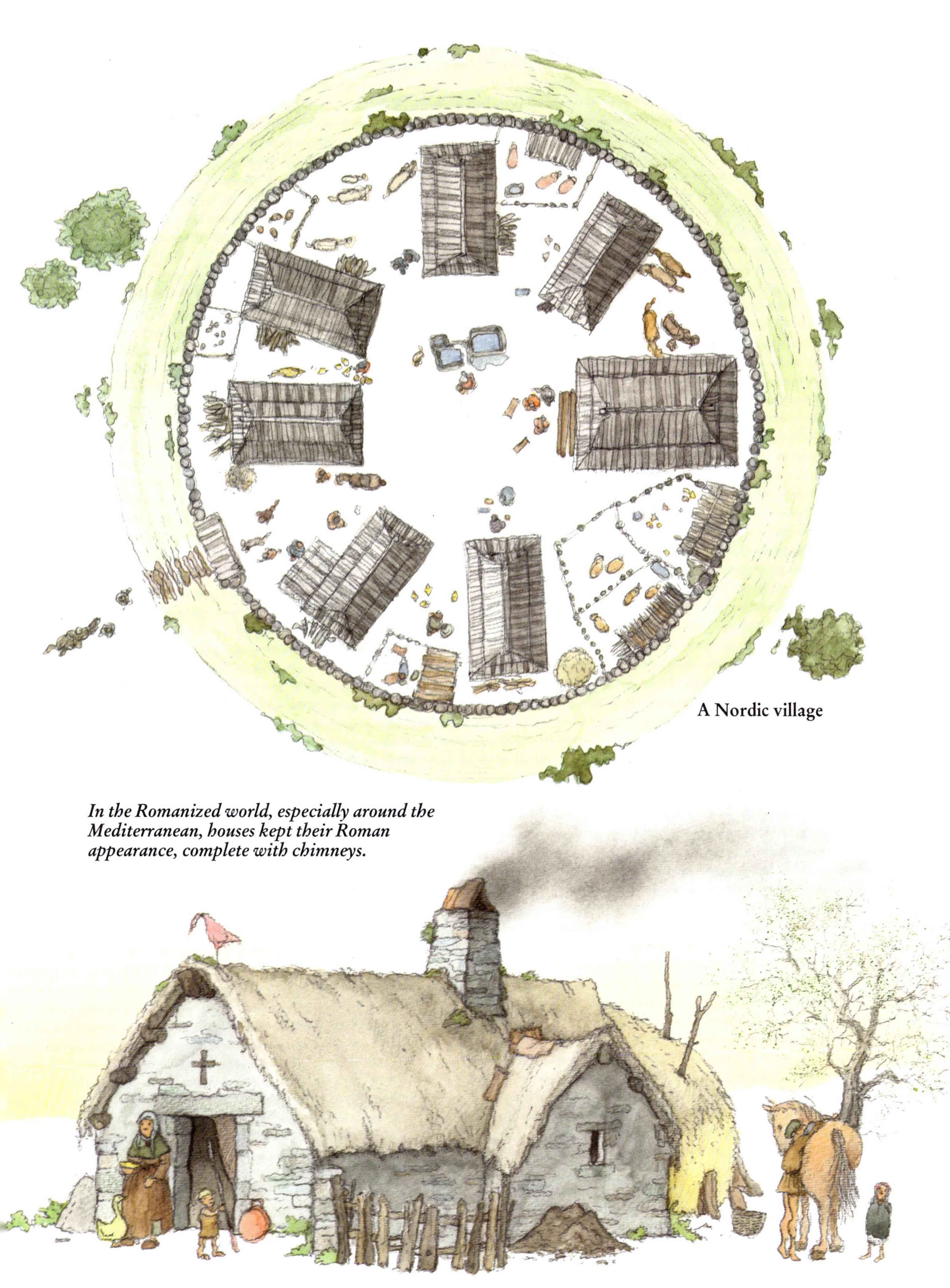

A Nordic village

In the Romanized world, especially around the
Mediterranean, houses kept their Roman
appearance, complete with chimneys.

The agricultural crisis, which was already under way when the Roman Empire was beginning to crumble, lasted for centuries and was accompanied by terrible plagues. The invasions uprooted whole peoples, greatly affecting their relationship to the land. The Goths and Lombards settled in northern Italy; the Swabians and Vandals in Andalusia in southern Spain, and the Franks in Gaul (modern France).

Systems of irrigation and land reclamation had fallen into disrepair and the land soon became devastated. The arrival of new migrating tribes made the recovery period even longer and more difficult.

The Germanic kings divided their conquered territories into fiefs, putting a trusted follower in charge of each fief. Farmers belonged to the fief in which they worked and they were not allowed to leave. No longer a slave, the farmer was a serf of the *glebe* (the land) and he had to farm the lord's land in addition to producing food for himself. In exchange for the *corvée* – unpaid labour on the lord's land – peasants were given small plots of land to grow their own vegetables and were allowed to keep certain grazing, hunting and fishing rights. Although they could take wood from uncultivated areas of the feud, a specified amount of all they produced, known as *gratuities*, had to go to the castle.

Whatever the peasant farmer or shepherd managed to put aside for the winter was always at risk of being seized by bands of robbers or the invading armies that constantly swept across Europe in search of power. The peasant farmer often had to become a soldier and defend the castle in which he had the right to seek refuge.

Because nearly all tools were made of wood, farm technology was slow to develop during feudal times. Grain was beaten with a flail, separated out from the lighter chaff by winnowing in the wind and then ground in a hand-powered mill.

Families lived on small, intensely cultivated plots of land around their houses. As the rigid Roman division of land gave way to haphazard fields determined by each household, the whole layout of the land changed.

The Germanic races, who had fewer slaves, were more interested than the Romans in developing tools that would make physical labour easier and more productive. Strong axes and saws were used for felling trees, while sharp sword blades were produced for war. With iron-rich land common in central Europe, and with the use of coal-fuelled forges equipped with bellows, great advances were made during this period in metal working.

Nestling at the foot of the castle walls, the feudal village included a row of artisans' workshops. There was a blacksmith, who shod horses and made chains; a woodworker and carpenter, who served as cart maker and cooper too; a tanner, who worked the leather to make clothes and armour; and a weaver.

Only in the large towns did artisans become independent craftsmen whose products were bought by the wealthy and even by kings. These skilled specialists were expert at gilding, working in copper and silver, sculpting marble and ivory and producing intricate mosaics and fine ironwork.

Although writing survived in the castles, it flourished mainly in the monasteries. Scribes spent long hours illuminating capital letters and filling entire pages with small, intricate illustrations. Because they frequently used red lead – *minium* – these pictures were called 'miniatures'. Kings, both at court and during their travels, were always accompanied by a scribe to whom they dictated letters and records of events.

When a piece of metal came out of the forge, red-hot, the blacksmith gripped it with tongs and hammered it into shape on the anvil. As soon as he was satisfied with the shape, he tempered it by plunging it into water. The sudden cooling made the iron stronger. The forge and the casting furnace were made of heat-resistant metals and were constantly blown with bellows to obtain maximum heat from the burning wood or coal.

Here we see two illuminated capital 'O's.

Byzantine-style gold and pearl necklaces were a speciality of many Italian jewellers.

The engraving of the scourging of Christ on this ivory plaque is simple and unsophisticated.

This is an example of the barbarian style of ironwork set with precious stones.

During this period trade suffered due to the low level of production. Although there was not much surplus farm produce for sale, the depopulated towns did not require great stores of provisions either. Farmers brought their goods into town, and each town set aside specific areas where produce from the country-side could be sold. In many towns the old Roman forum evolved into the market-place.

Along with other Roman achievements, the road system also fell into bad disrepair. Long journeys were constantly interrupted so that goods did not travel much more than 40 kilometres a day. Traders had to cross different fiefdoms, each one imposing its own duties and tolls making the cost of transporting goods from one town to another very high.

The passes over the Alps had also fallen into disrepair. Traders travelling between Italy and Germany had to go down the Rhône Valley and the Ligurian coast, making the journey three times longer than before. Although sea transport was less costly than land transport, it was not always possible. When it was possible, the merchant had to entrust his wares to unknown people which was often very risky.

Communications were better in the Near East, where the Arab world was growing and the Byzantine Empire still flourished. Trade with the East, though not as strong as it had once been, was still vigorous, and from the cities of Damascus, Mosul and Baghdad came luxurious cloths named after their origins – damask, muslin and baldachin.

To avoid the confusion of different currencies,
payment was often made in goods. At the same
time that Charlemagne in Europe was reforming
the monetary system and imposing the use of
silver only, the Arabs were introducing a new
gold coin. This was the dinar – worth 0.002 of a
kilogram of gold.

The corn stored in the castle
granaries constituted the
wealth of the feudal lord. It
was used for bartering and for
paying the tribute to the
sovereign.

Roman influences survived in fashion although clothing was now influenced by the elaborate decorative styles of the East and the Byzantine world, as well as by the simpler styles and thick woollen garments of northern Europe.

It was at this time that breeches became a basic part of male dress, especially among the working classes. Leather breeches were cut tight around the legs, while cloth breeches were pulled tight with laces. A knee- or calf-length tunic or doublet, which was tucked up under the belt when its wearer was working, was worn over the breeches. In winter, a cape was worn diagonally over the tunic, leaving the right arm free. Those who could afford them wore soft leather shoes laced at the front.

Women dressed in long, colourfully dyed tunics. The earth and vegetable dyes which they used were fixed with acidic substances such as urine. Women wore their hair long, often down to their thighs.

The use of two different colours in a person's clothing, usually yellow and blue or red and green, originated in the north. This fashion, which spread throughout medieval Europe, was adopted by town criers, standard bearers and soldiers.

Byzantine crowns, studded with pearls and precious stones, influenced the headwear of the new Germanic aristocrats. Although Germanic headwear was often made of iron, it was decorated with gold and jewels.

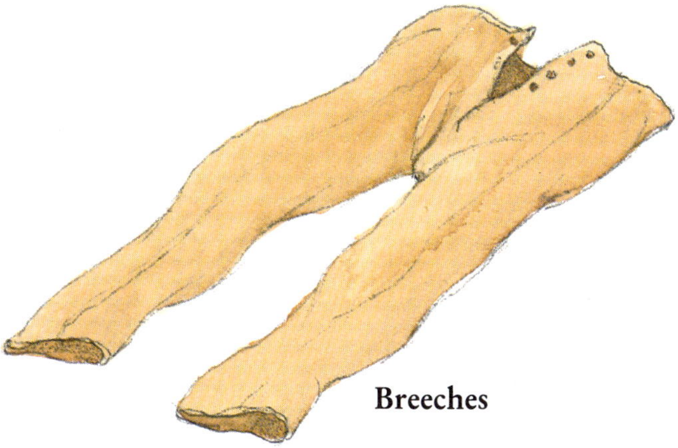

Breeches

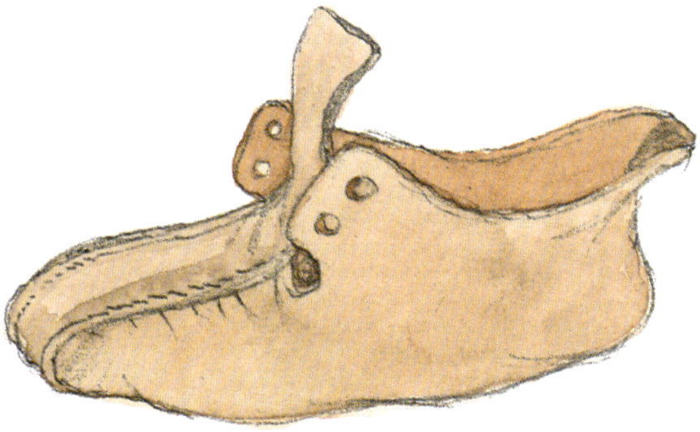

Leather shoes

During this period, the vestments used in Christian rites showed Byzantine influences. Byzantine symbolism and grandeur became part of Western tradition.

The clothes worn by various classes

Lady of the Manor

Merchant

Peasant

Apprentice

The wheel saw little development under the Romans and ordinary wagons still used solid wheels which exerted great friction on the axles. Although attempts were made to solve this by covering the axles with leather and bronze, the real solution lay in two developments from northern Europe. The first development was lighter wheels with spokes and the second was the use of bearings in the form of small wooden rollers placed between the axle and the hub. Iron rims, sometimes studded with nails for a better grip, lengthened the life of the wheel, but they did so much damage to streets that some towns banned them. As a result, leather rims were adopted for town driving. Meanwhile, the horse's harness was improved, with shafts replacing the single pole.

Over the years the fine Roman roads deteriorated. Farmers removed the paving stones to use in the foundations of their buildings, leaving only an earth surface, which actually made travelling by horseback easier. To avoid paying tolls, riders tended to take roundabout routes, no matter how long and tortuous. Because of this, a new road network gradually emerged that was far more irregular than the precise, straight lines of the old Roman roads.

Shipbuilding continued in the tradition of the skilled axemen of the Baltic and North Seas. Ships' hulls were made of overlapping planks fastened with iron pegs. As ship design improved rapidly, first the Irish and then the Vikings from Scandinavia became superb navigators. The Vikings explored as far as Greenland and the northern shores of America.

Deforestation increased the amount of land that could be farmed. Tree trunks were floated downstream to shipyards at seaports.

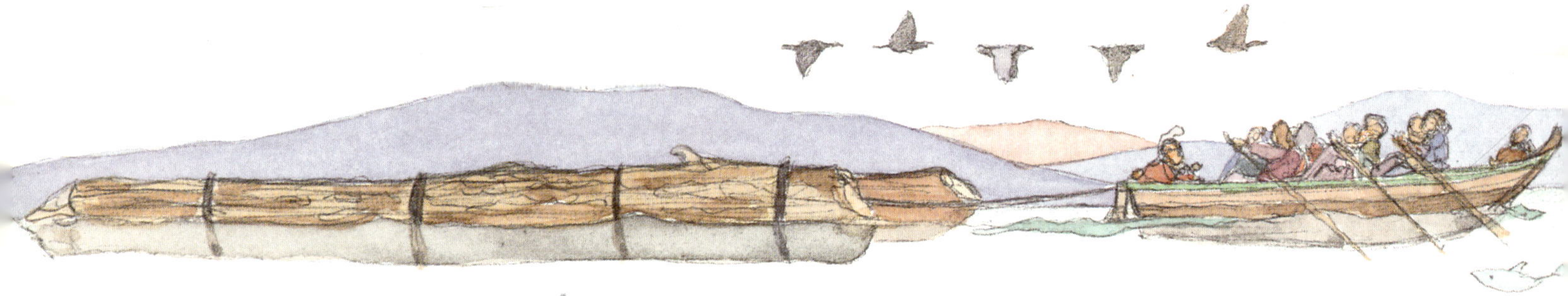

Sledges with an articulated harness were the traditional means of transport and remained in use for many centuries.

The wheelbarrow (right), which is based on the lever principle, was so efficient in increasing a person's work capacity that it is still in common use today.

A Viking ship

As agriculture gradually recovered and farms improved, the population increased, making the techniques of storing and preserving food even more important. Although each area kept its old traditions, various new ways of making cheese and salting meat and fish became widespread. In order to sell their fish, the people of northern Europe gutted and cleaned them, then either packed them closely in barrels, like herring, or dried them, like cod. Preserving in oil or brine was more common in the south.

In the Germanic world, there were still no real towns, only villages, like Charlemagne's capital, Aquisgranum – known today as Aachen. As Germanic society became more urban, building techniques had to be developed.

The real builders of the age were the Arabs, who acquired Byzantine building skills and developed them further, in fanciful structures topped with domes. Cordoba, the capital of the Spanish caliphate, became a magnificent city with 400 mosques and a population of half a million. Before AD 1000, Baghdad, on the River Tigris, with miles of street-lighting, was the largest city in the world.

The process of reconstruction in Europe after the invasions was greatly helped by the monasteries which had preserved and handed down Roman technology. As a result, the monasteries became the centres of research and experimentation in many spheres of knowledge.

Craftwork, especially in metal, required heat for energy. Because Europe was still mostly covered by huge forests, wood was in plentiful supply. Although the widespread clearing of forests that took place to provide wood created new farmlands, it did not allow time or space for new trees to grow. Because wood had to be found farther and farther afield at increasing expense, coal mining developed.

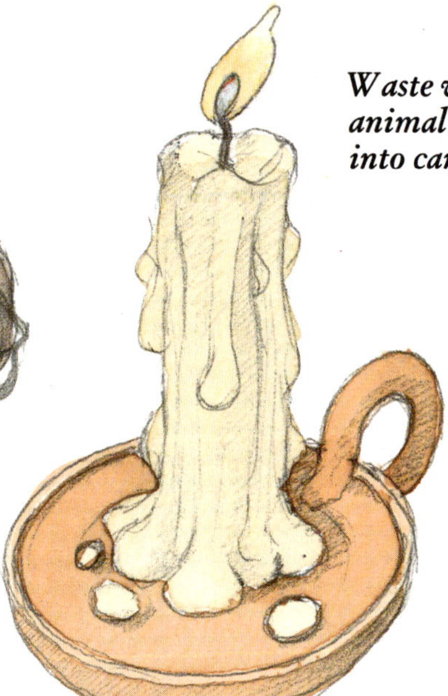

Waste vegetables and animal fats were made into candles.

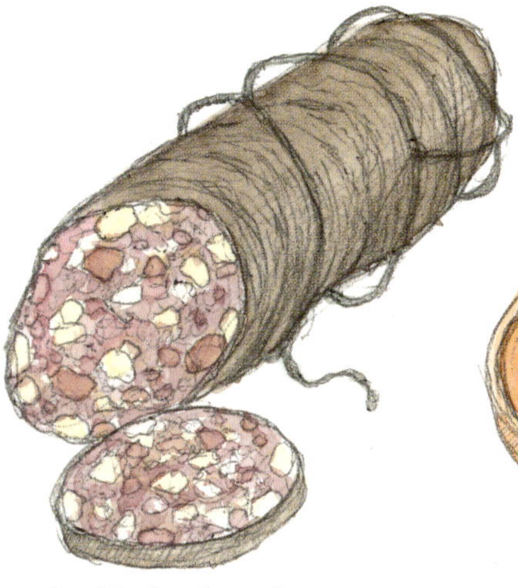

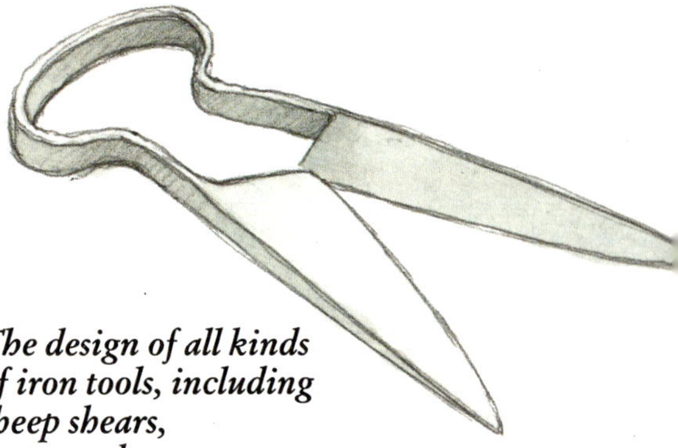

The design of all kinds of iron tools, including sheep shears, improved.

Valuable foods such as meat and fish could be preserved in salt or smoked.

Monasteries resembled highly organized villages, with a church, a library, a refectory and a cloister in the centre. The cells where the monks slept surrounded the cloister, while workshops of every description were at the back.

To turn wood into charcoal, branches were heaped over a fireplace and completely covered with earth, except for an opening left at the top. The fire was then lit. As the slowly burning wood dried out, carbon, in the form of charcoal, was left.

The great strength of the Germanic and Slavic troops lay not so much in deployment and tactics as in the speed and force and skill of their attack, as well as their courage in combat. While the Roman cavalry had served only as a back-up force, horses now became central to warfare. With the invention of stirrups, the rider was seated more safely, could move more freely, and also had a foothold for support when he threw a spear or attacked with an axe or sword. Although the long sword was the most widely used weapon, arms and armour had not yet become standardized; they varied from group to group and some of them even incorporated certain Roman features. Contemporary records describe particularly ferocious bands of warriors who wore helmets shaped like the heads of bears, wolves, dogs and other animals. These helmets were based on old ritual masks originally used for the festivities of the supreme god, Woden, also known as Odin.

Thick clothing and furs were needed in the harsh northern climate. Although saddles were considered a luxury in battle, horses were protected from the cold by saddle-cloths.

Armour made of interlocking iron rings was copied from the Romans. Because few could afford such armour, a breastplate of thick leather or fur was more commonly used.

61

The Middle Ages

The Germanic Empire never really succeeded in uniting all of western Europe under one king. Its greatest enemy was the papacy, which occasionally allied itself with external forces who opposed the Empire. The papacy also supported internal forces – the more highly developed cities, which wanted to rule themselves, and were therefore determined to dissolve the Empire's unit. This centuries-long struggle began with the battle over the appointment of bishops in these cities.

The Empire managed to survive only because of the tribute that was raised from the richer cities of the Rhineland and northern Italy. These areas, which had little liking for imperial authority and even less liking for the

Emperors were elected, often amid fierce rivalry and corruption, by the upper nobility. These nobles handed down both titles and possessions within their families. In this way a hereditary aristocracy was established.

The merchant class, which grew more and more wealthy as trade increased, often allied itself with the bishop. The trade guilds and corporations became powerful bodies with a strong voice in the government of the city.

Unity among the various European states was occasionally achieved during the Crusades, when all kingdoms united against a common enemy, the Saracens. As free commercial enterprise increased in importance, fighting the Saracens became less of a concern.

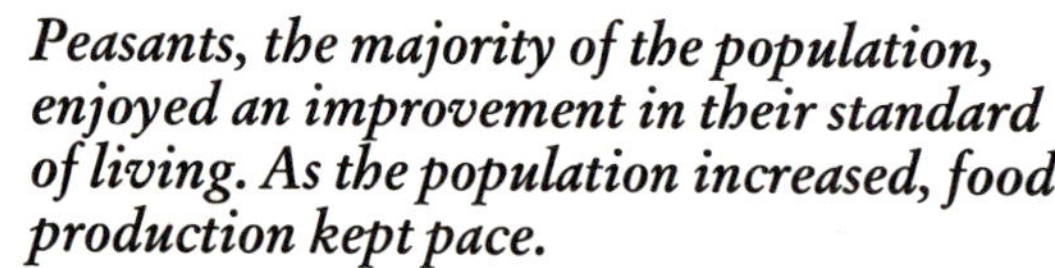

Peasants, the majority of the population, enjoyed an improvement in their standard of living. As the population increased, food production kept pace.

feudal lords and lord-bishops, fought on many occasions together against the imperial army.

Because of the rivalry between the various communes, republics, and free cities, the sovereign always had plenty of room to manoeuvre. The fierce battles which raged within these political groups resulted in the emergence of two opposing forces. One force was aristocratic and loyal to the emperor, the other was made up of rich entrepreneurs and merchants who supported the papacy.

The governments of the free communes had to strike a balance between rival factions. Laws regulating life in the city were proclaimed, and a council to each city elected the supreme magistrates. Associated with these magistrates in some Italian city-states was someone called a *capitano del popolo*, an outsider with no direct interests in the city who led the common people and looked after their interests. The third most influential person in the city was the bishop.

The wealth of the city depended on the professional skills and energy of the emerging middle class. The fine new buildings of this period were constructed for this new section of the population.

Medieval society, at its peak in the 13th century, expressed its vitality in a tremendous burst of building. Roman towns were rebuilt, enlarged and circled with new walls that included outlying villages. With the great increase in both population and wealth, new towns sprang up in rural areas. In the centre of these towns were magnificent cathedrals and town halls. These buildings symbolized the independence and power of the guilds which competed with each other in their construction of every one of these churches and public buildings.

Even small towns, which were occupied mostly by artisans and tradesmen, were fortified with bastions, walls and gates. In mountainous areas, hilltop sites were chosen because they were easier to defend. The rural population took refuge in the towns when there were raids from other communes or when invasion threatened from the East or from the sea. The rural nobility owned castles set in woodlands and gardens in the country, and tall towers that were half house and half castle in the towns. They claimed their rights in the towns as well as in the country. Rival families with bands of followers often met in the streets to fight out their endless feuds.

Apart from the large market square, the public areas of medieval towns and cities were no larger than was needed for pedestrians and traffic. Following the natural contours of the land, the streets were often tortuous and steep. This proved to be a great advantage in defending a town against any invaders who had managed to get through the gates.

Ownership of town land was carefully allotted, and buildings had to stand in the space given to them. Because lots (or plots of land) were long and narrow, the shops that lined the main streets had their storehouses and workshops at the back and living quarters above.

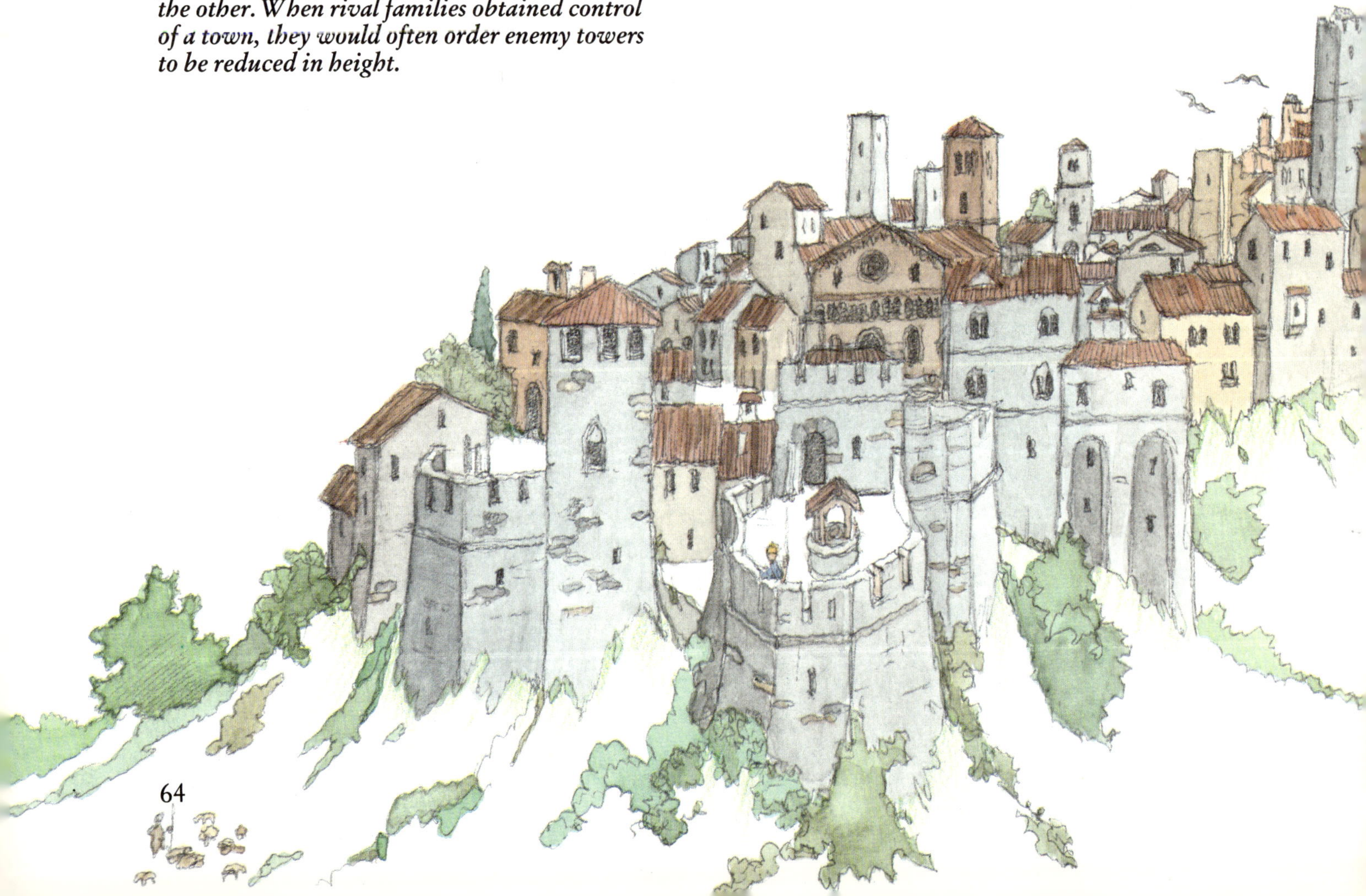

Along the busiest streets in town were the shops of craftsmen and merchants. The most desirable sites were those that opened on to the market square. The same house-with-shop design was found all over Europe. They combined Roman and Norman features.

Houses were enlarged by building overhanging upper storeys. Every so often an official on horseback rode down the streets with a spear held up crosswise to make sure that these storeys did not encroach on the space that by law had to be left between houses.

Much of the remarkable economic and cultural expansion in Europe between about 950 and 1300 was due to improvements in farming. Once vast areas of land had been deforested and prepared for tilling, the peasants were assigned plots in exchange for fixed *corvées*, which enabled them to grow more than enough produce for their own needs. By having goods for barter, the peasants were in a position to make money which, in turn, allowed them to buy goods once available only to the nobility. In order to produce more, the farmers needed better tools, and this created business for the metalworkers. If additional farm-hands were needed, the farmer and his wife often used their own children instead of hiring help. Under a patriarchal family system, the population boomed and once again an agricultural tradition developed. Various specialities and styles of farming, such as seed selection, grafting and crop rotation, emerged.

The invention of the ploughshare, meant that only one plough was necessary. Long, narrow strips of land were given to individual farmers on either side of a central road. As dwellings grew up along this road, the medieval farming village evolved.

*Developments in the crafts benefited agriculture.
Examples are: the chest harness with a padded
collar for draught horses, and the articulated
plough with an iron mould-board, which made
it possible to plough more deeply.*

*The pig was the basis of the diet of farming
families throughout Europe. It provided both
meat and fat. Other basic items included bread
and traditional alcoholic drinks, wine in the
south and beer in the north.*

*In Mediterranean countries where the dry land
had only a shallow layer of soil, deep ploughing
was not necessary. Central and eastern Europe,
with plenty of water and rich, clay soil, became
the great cereal producers.*

The growth of both the population and agricultural productivity resulted in a shift in the work force from the land into different trades. The farmers' increased purchasing power created a new demand for craftwork, providing artisans with more income. During the 13th century, numerous self-employed artisans, by now rich and influential, organized themselves into corporations, or *guilds*, to protect their interest and keep a check on what the various workshops were producing. Because the different trades now had to be recognized by their respective guilds, it was no longer possible simply to set up as an artisan such as a chemist or a weaver. The guilds issued laws which regulated the quality of production and decided the terms on which producers could share the market. Representing a considerable force, the guilds had a strong financial and political voice in the running of the towns.

Every trade had its jealously guarded secrets. Unfortunately, this form of self-protection tended to discourage new ideas and inventions. The idea of a *patent*, which ensured that anyone could use a new invention by paying a certain sum to the inventor, came much later.

Most of the workers in guild workshops were day labourers who often lived and ate in the same house as their employer. To complete their training, *apprentices* went from one workshop to another and from town to town. When they had finished their training, they had to produce their *masterpiece*, an object that met the standards of their guild. Not until they had proved their professional skill in this way were they recognized as *masters*.

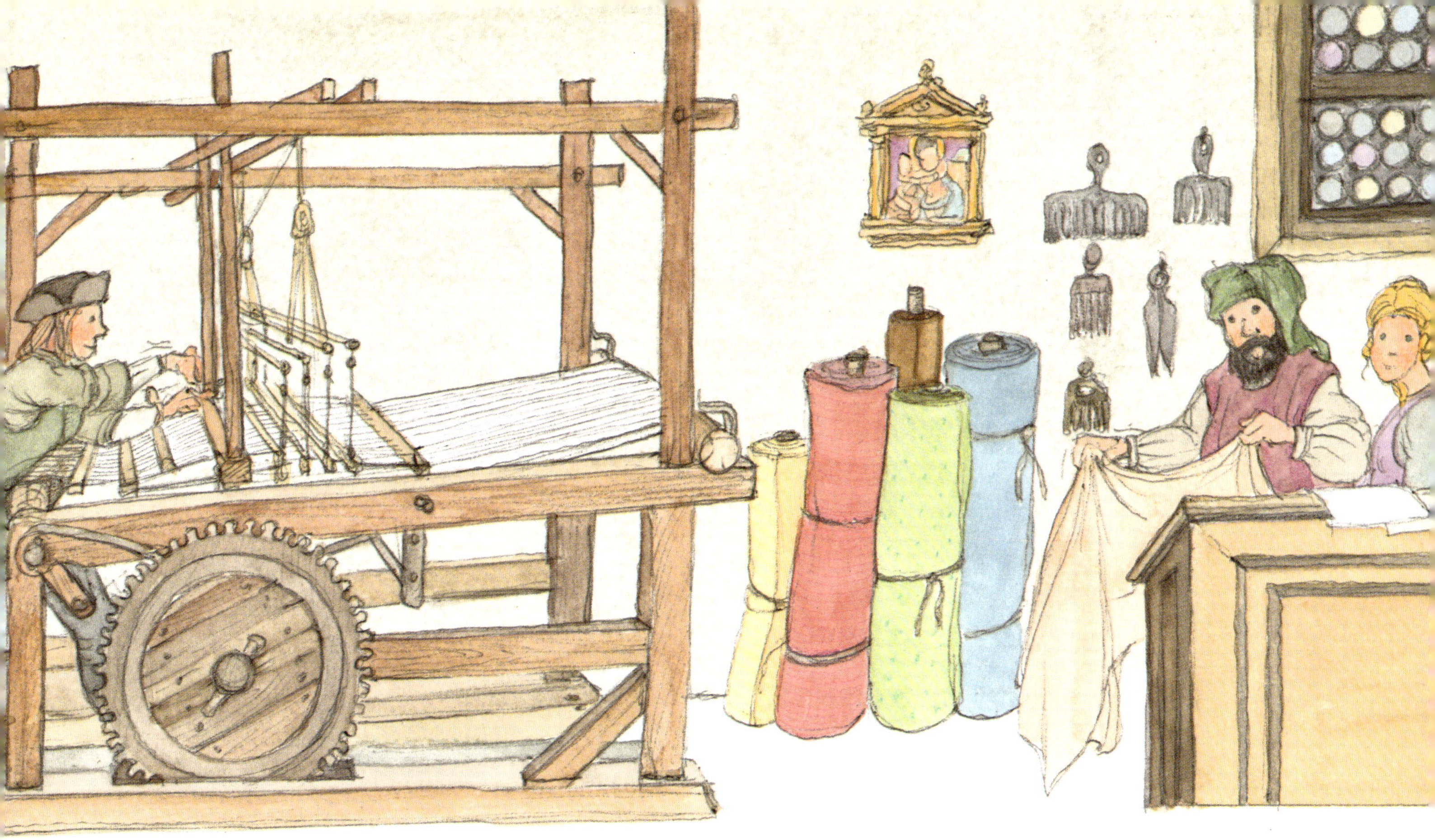

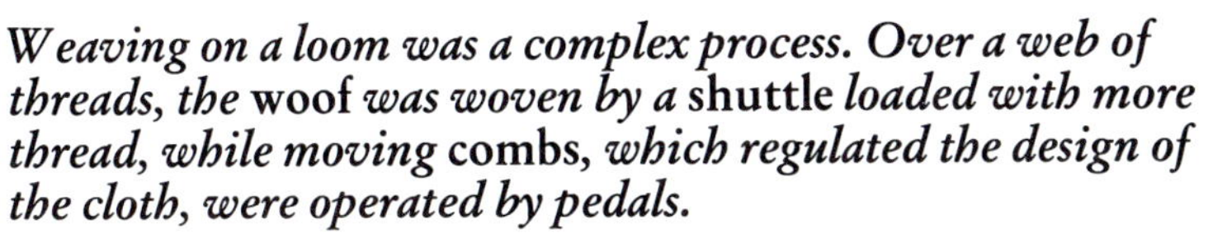

Weaving on a loom was a complex process. Over a web of threads, the woof was woven by a shuttle loaded with more thread, while moving combs, which regulated the design of the cloth, were operated by pedals.

Few farmers favoured the water mill (left), even though it was more efficient and produced finer flour than that ground at home with mortar and pestle or in a small domestic mill. The explanation may be that the feudal lord who built and ran the mill imposed a flour-milling tax.

Distilling alcohol from wine (right) required some knowledge of chemistry, and needed special equipment that only pharmacists and monks possessed. Such alcohol was thought of as the 'essential element' of the wine from which it had been distilled and was known as aqua vitae, 'water of life'. Fermented cereals were distilled in a similar way to produce whisky.

The merchant class became powerful in the free cities. They were no longer mere shopkeepers who bought and sold goods that happened to be brought to their town. They had become large-scale entrepreneurs, shipowners and patrons of fairs and markets, and their warehouses were filled with goods of all kinds.

After the Crusades, closer links were established with the East, and this reopened a large market. Seaports, their livelihood based on trade, had supplied ships and money to the crusading knights. The silk trade route, open once more, led from the port of Rostov on the Black Sea, through Samarkand, and on to the Mongol Empire and Peking. Venice, one of the greatest cities of Europe and the major port on the route to the East, was isolated and protected by its lagoon. Governed as an independent republic, it reaped great profits from its maritime trade. In northern Europe, trade on the Baltic was monopolized by the cities of the German Hanseatic League. German merchants established major trading centres in London, Bruges, Flanders, and in Novgorod, Russia.

Because of poor roads and the expense of tolls and duties, transport by land was a problem. Successful merchants managed to negotiate special trading deals in exchange for money loans to local lords and they made use of the trade fairs which were traditionally free.

Nevertheless, most transportation of valuable goods was still risky and merchants made sure that they had either solid capital behind them, or that money – provided by other merchants – was available to them. Banks evolved from these needs, both to look after the fortunes of their clients, and to lend money to trustworthy clients. The major merchants, with their own money benches – 'bank' comes from the Italian word *banco*, or 'bench' – were also bankers. Florence and Siena were particularly renowned as banking cities.

Letters of credit from a well-known bank were as valuable as money. Because there were certain Church laws against lending money, or usury, careful formulas had to be worked out to determine acceptable interest rates on loans.

The economy of naval republics such as Genoa and Venice in Italy, and of the German Hanseatic cities with their capital at Lübeck, was based entirely on trade. The centre of commerce between Venice and Lübeck was originally at Bruges, in Flanders, but it had to be moved to Antwerp when the port at Bruges started to silt up. Venetians always had spices and silks from the East for sale, while Lübeck offered wools and Russian furs. Ships from the south sailed with cargoes of fruit, oil, wine and woollen cloth, while ships arrived from the north laden with minerals, fish and wool.

As the textile industry flourished, 13th-century tailors worked with fine wools, soft silks, cottons light as gauze, heavy velvets and as well as luxury fabrics from the newly reopened Eastern markets.

Fashions varied from country to country. In Italy, women wore a long, tight tunic with clinging sleeves and a loose overgarment with sleeves that widened at the wrist to reveal the different fabric and colour of the tunic beneath. Towards the end of the 13th century, women began to cut their hair.

French women wore a light tunic, with tight sleeves and an embroidered neckline, under a flowing coat which was belted at the waist and had sleeves that reached to the ground.

Women in the north imitated Italian and French fashions, the difference being that their overgarment had side slits to reveal the tunic underneath and did not have sleeves. On their heads they wore a stylized crown with a piece of material called a wimple hanging from it which framed the face.

Men also wore two tunics, with massive leather belts decorated with metal studs. The tights they now wore instead of breeches had no pockets, so that wallets or purses hung from the belt or were slung over the shoulder.

Fashions in the 14th century became even more elaborate. To 'streamline' their bodies, women's clothing became tighter under the breasts and swept down into long trains.

Typical hairstyles of the Middle Ages

The variety of materials, colours and accessories worn by an individual depended on social class. For example, the 'common people' were not allowed to wear colours such as scarlet, and certain shades of blue and green. Workmen used a certain kind of cloth, friars used another kind, and servants used cloth with striped bands.

With Europe divided, and Saracens to be found on all its southern shores, pirates roamed the once safe and peaceful Mediterranean. As merchant ships had to learn to defend themselves, the difference between warships and trading vessels disappeared. Small fortified 'castles' (the forecastle and quarterdeck) were built at bow and stern. It was ships like these that King Louis IX of France hired when he led the crusade of 1268.

Spanish merchant ships introduced the lateen sail, which had probably been used on Byzantine ships originally. This was a modified version of the square sail, with the yardarm slanted and the bottom edge of the sail shortened in order to catch contrary winds. This meant that it was possible to sail against the wind. The single flat rudder mounted at the stern replaced twin steering oars so that now ships could be steered easily from a seat on the quarterdeck. To counterbalance a second mast that was added towards the bow, a third mast was added on the quarterdeck. With all these improvements, ships were able to navigate the open seas more safely. In fact, no sooner had the Islamic threat been met and dealt with once and for all, than Christopher Columbus set sail for America.

A caravel

A Mediterranean galley

*Riding on horseback was still the fastest form of
land travel. Saddles, stirrups, reins, bits, spurs
and harnesses were all improved to make riding
safer and more comfortable. Posting stations
were set up along major roads, where riders
could change horses, have them reshod, or
simply stop for refreshment.*

The economic boom under the feudal system and in the free cities stimulated research into ways to increase production of goods and improve the quality of what was produced. Deforestation and land reclamation over vast areas, such as the Black Forest and the Danube Valley, created a need for large numbers of axes, saws and mould-boards. During this period, tools became increasingly efficient, and advances were made in forging and tempering steel. Water energy was harnessed to power hammers by attaching cams to the shaft of the wheel, which raised the hammer and let it drop back on the anvil. This method, which made rolling iron easier, was also used to produce pestles for papermaking and presses for fulling (cleansing and thickening) cloth.

Animal power, especially horse power, became more effective with the development of the chest harness and stirrups. While the old leather collars could suffocate a horse, the new stuffed collar made full use of the horse's strong pectoral (chest) muscles.

When Rome collapsed, many ancient skills were lost, especially in the manufacture of textiles, glassware and ceramics. Because these old skills survived in the Byzantine and Islamic worlds, they were reintroduced to Europe by the Arabs.

The Benedictine monasteries played a fundamental role as research centres for all forms of industry as well as agriculture. No large abbey was without a cellar, brewery, lime kiln, mill, or workshops. The monks, from the herbalist to the artisan and from the launderer to the tanner, practised their trades here. Monasteries spread quickly, while keeping close contacts with each other. Any new inventions introduced in monasteries therefore spread rapidly all over Europe.

The new padded horse collar

An iron ploughshare which ploughed deeply

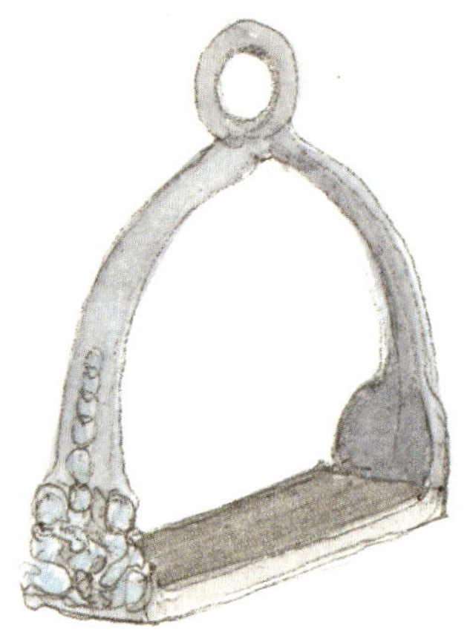

Roads were barely passable for animal-drawn vehicles, so saddles and stirrups, essential for comfort, came into common use.

A water hammer

Just as Europe was becoming stable after centuries of conflict between Germanic kings, a fresh wave of invasions of Vikings, Magyars and Saracens broke from the north and east. Once again Europe was plunged into long and exhausting wars, and whole armies were occupied for years in the East during the Crusades. The political agreements that followed led to a division of the continent into separate, rival kingdoms such as France and England, which were at each other's throats for a hundred years. Even the free cities, communes, and principalities within the kingdoms often fought each other over land, money or political power.

Every feudal lord kept his own small army of guards. This was increased in time of war by the vassals to whom the lord had granted privileges and concessions.

From childhood, the male children of the nobility were trained in arms. The eldest son would succeed his father as lord and chief of the army. The other sons had to use their fighting ability to make their own way in the world; they would serve one of the greater lords, who would reward them with fiefs of their own.

A knight was armed with a lance over 4 metres long, an iron-studded mace, an axe and a broadsword.

A crossbow

A bolt

In the age of chivalry, knights championed Christianity, justice and honour; those chivalrous ideals were the subject of epic poetry and heroic tales for centuries. Knights swore loyalty unto death to their code of honour.

The knight wore mail and plate armour. The plumes on his helmet and decoration on his shield made him a gallant sight indeed.

# Absolute Monarchs

England and France, at war with each other in the 14th century, eventually established their respective kingdoms, while the German empire splintered into small independent duchies and principalities. Taking advantage of this constant turmoil, the leading families in the free communes gained control.

After the death in 1558 of the last great emperor, Charles V, Europe was split into a number of different states, some large and some small, each governed by its own monarch. The only republic to survive was

In return for their homage and loyalty, aristocrats acquired many privileges. The most important government positions went to the king's powerful ministers – clever diplomats who best understood how to influence their sovereign's political decisions.

Armies were made up of mercenaries and commanded by professional officers. They were in constant active service and became stable military units.

Lawyers and bureaucrats were in a class above the common people.

Venice, with a second republic, Holland, soon to develop in the Low Countries. Although the Pope was also secular sovereign over his own recognized Church state, the Reformation challenged his spiritual authority. Europe was soon deeply divided between Catholic and Protestant states. Religious wars were the inevitable result. Territorial and religious disputes, and social unrest all led to continuing armed conflict.

Production and creativity in the Middle Ages had generally been a communal effort. Now individuals who were to become famous as artists and scholars began to emerge from the guilds. Beginning in Italy, the great cultural revival, known as the Renaissance, ('rebirth') spread throughout Europe. Michelangelo, Leonardo and Raphael emerged as artists who contributed greatly to this period of history. Other equally famous Renaissance figures are Columbus and Galileo.

During the same period, great poets and playwrights, such as Ariosto, Shakespeare, Tasso and Molière were writing works that have helped people through the ages to examine and understand human nature. Even the 'art' of politics was developed into a complex theory by Machiavelli in his book *The Prince*, while Castiglione's *The Book of the Courtier* set a universal example of elegance and good manners. Great technological achievements such as the advances in seafaring, mining, agriculture, weaving and various crafts were also important.

Artists and scientists at a Renaissance court

This great rebirth of culture in Europe followed a period of crisis and decadence, a period which had been marked by famine and plague for most of the 14th century.

The sense of rebirth, which spread from Italy to France and from there throughout Europe, also had a great impact on architecture. The rediscovery of the Greco-Roman past and of classical styles both took place during the Renaissance. Ideal cities were planned and although these were based on abstract theories of style, certain practical improvements, such as using space wisely, were also taken into account. Medieval cities, with their maze-like streets had been criticized for being dingy and unhealthy. They were now replaced by open spaces, squares and great wide streets lined with fine houses.

Dynasties, both large and small, enjoyed absolute power. This meant that it was possible to build palaces the likes of which had not been seen since Roman times. The aristocracy too, built grand houses decorated with superb works of art. Florence, with its splendid buildings and country villas, which were like small palaces, housed some fine examples of the architectural renaissance.

Farther north, Gothic architecture remained fashionable for centuries. Techniques of half-timbering were developed to such an extent that woodworking became as decorative as embroidery, while in the Low Countries, (modern-day Netherlands, Belgium and Luxembourg), where wood was less plentiful, handsome buildings were built of brick.

The greatest changes in urban planning came later, in the 17th century, when ambitious development programmes were undertaken in Rome under Pope Urban VIII, in Amsterdam and in London after the Great Fire of 1666.

The Gothic tradition in building in northern Europe lasted for centuries. The Tudor style in England coexisted with the new architecture of Inigo Jones who was greatly inspired by the Italian renaissance.

After the Great Fire in 1666, London was completely rebuilt in brick and stone. Many of the more important buildings, were designed by Christopher Wren in the Italian classical style.

The half-timbered houses lining the main thoroughfares of German towns often had their own names. These were taken from the name of the family who lived there, from the use the public made of the building or from the sign over the entrance.

 After the turbulent years of the 14th century, the burden of recovery, once again fell on the farmers. It was not until the 16th century, and in some places even later, that agriculture came into its own again. When the peasants in Germany, who lived under difficult conditions, rebelled, they were harshly and quickly suppressed by both secular and Church authorities.

Conditions were much better in the Low Countries. As the population grew, more land was made available through painstaking reclamation from the sea. This was done by using an elaborate process of drainage and dike building. Those who worked on these projects acquired part-ownership of the reclaimed land, where intensive small-scale farming techniques proved to be very effective. The Dutch farmers, now as rich and respected as other working classes, were the first farmers in Europe to be represented on property councils.

By careful management of their pastures, the Dutch became expert in cheese production.

The building of windmills became widespread in the 15th century, especially in the flat areas of northern Europe. The power generated by the windmills was used to suck water away from the polders, (marshland). Fertile farmland was thereby created.

After the colonization of America, previously unknown crops such as beans and potatoes were introduced in Europe. These products, high in calories, soon became staple items in the European diet.

The invention of the printing press in the mid-15th century not only revolutionized the spread of information, but it was also part of a new manufacturing process which grew quickly. By the beginning of the 16th century, only fifty years after the invention of the printing press, some eight million books had been printed – more than had been copied by hand since the earliest days of writing.

Printing was highly specialized work. It involved making, or casting, movable characters, composing pages from the movable type and preparing the paper before the actual process of printing with a hand press began. Books were then bound and the fine leather bindings decorated. Consequently, related trades also developed to produce, for example, paper and special inks that would not smudge.

The production of paper, which was invented by the Chinese and brought to Europe by the Arabs, became an important business only after the invention of the printing press. Paper was made by soaking vegetable fibres such as flax or cotton in water and then pulping them, recovering the waste for later use. The remaining paste, which was filtered from the water, was spread on frames that were the same size as the required sheet size and was then compressed. After a thorough drying, the sheets were ready for the printer.

Glass production expanded greatly during this period, especially in cities such as Venice, where the island of Murano soon became world-famous for its glass. The glassblower's tools were simple: an iron pipe to blow through and shape the molten glass and an iron support which, when applied red-hot to the glass object, kept it malleable enough to be worked at with tongs and shears. Fine glassware depended on the skill of the glassblower.

With the spread of copper engraving, pictures by famous artists now became more widely known. Printing from an engraved copperplate was based on the same technique as printing the written word; the plate was inked with a roller and then pressed against the paper in a hand press.

Pulped fibres soaked in water and ground with pestles produced the paste for papermaking. Although the pestles were operated by a handle, in larger businesses, a water wheel was used. At the far right of the illustration is the frame on which the paste was spread to make a sheet of paper.

At the heart of the glassmaker's workshop were the casting furnace for melting the raw materials – sodium carbonate and sand – and the reheating furnace used for joining the different parts of the finished product. A variety of earthenware or copper moulds completed the glassmaker's equipment.

In the years following Charlemagne's reform of the monetary system, the silver *denarius* was reduced in value as it became lighter in weight. This was due in part to the difficulty of finding enough silver to meet the growing demand. Because different communes, principalities and republics produced coins in their own mints, differently weighted currency appeared, none of which bore any relationship to the *libra*, the standard pound weight for gold and silver. The need for a more stable coinage, already felt in the mid-13th century, resulted in the Florentine gold florin and the Venetian gold ducat, both of which were soon in use all over Europe. The importance of gold became apparent by the 16th century, when the florin, which was originally worth one *lira*, escalated to a value of seven *lire*. To re-establish some sort of stability, the gold *scudo* was minted.

Only with the financial backing of the now enormously wealthy banks were the great expeditions to India and the West Indies possible. These voyages were undertaken to find treasure and cheap gold, as the Spanish did in Mexico and Peru and the Portuguese did in the African coast.

Exploration led to colonization, which in turn created an extensive and very profitable trading network that spanned the continents. Spanish traders sailed their galleons from Acapulco in Mexico to Manila in the Philippines, where they exchanged their cargoes of silver for silk. Sugar-cane, once grown on the Mediterranean coasts, was introduced into Brazil by the Portuguese. Because the new plantations were worked by slaves forcibly exported from Africa, the slave trade became a flourishing business once again.

Cinnamon

Pepper

Cloves

Nutmeg

Poppyseed

Ginger

Saffron

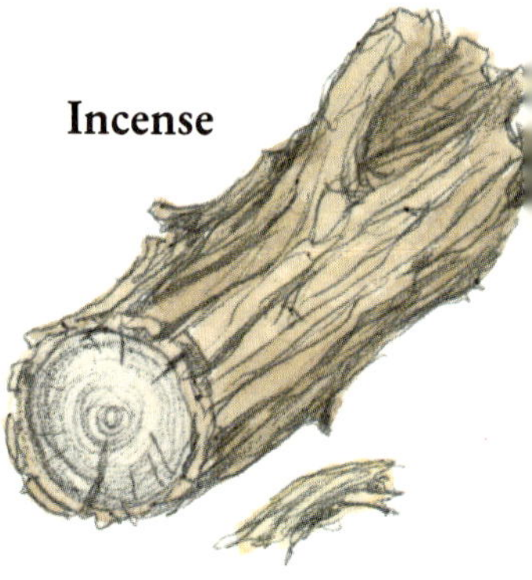

Incense

Lorenzo the Magnificent

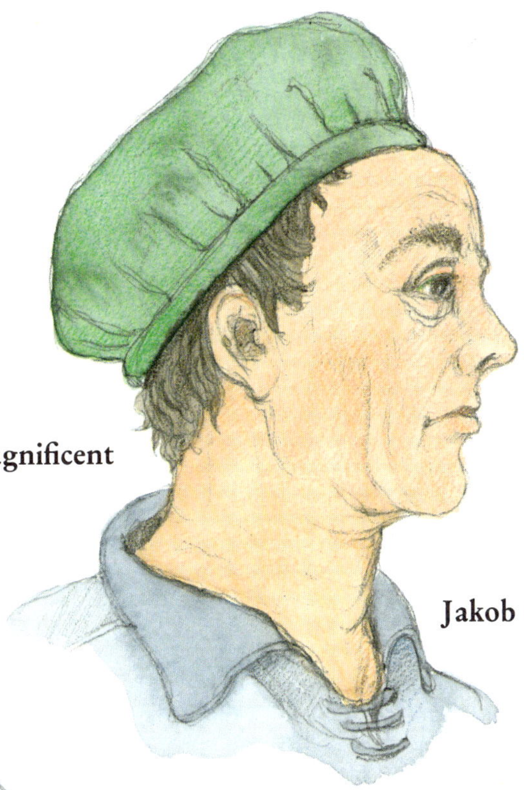

Jakob II

*The economic strength of the banks had a political impact. In Florence,
the Medici family (Lorenzo the Magnificent) established first a
signoria, or lordship, then a Grand Duchy. They also provided France
with two queens and the Church with a number of popes. In Augsburg,
Germany, the Fugger Family (Jakob II) even helped the Emperor
Charles V financially when he was having trouble paying his troops.*

*Here a money-changer
is weighing money on
scales. Worn-out coins
were bought by weight
and melted down.*

During the Middle Ages it was fashionable for women to wear dresses with trains. Although Renaissance women no longer wore trains, they started to wear the Spanish *vertugado*, which was originally just an under-skirt widened at the bottom by means of whalebone ribs. In France, however, the vertugado soon evolved into a great drum held up by a metal hoop around the hips, and waists were made tiny with painfully constricting corsets. In contrast, headgear became less elaborate, with the hair worn short or done up in a fine net.

Shirts became standard for men; slightly curled collars gradually becoming more elaborate and finally evolving into the starched *ruff*. Breeches were now gathered over stockings either above or below the knee, and like the sleeves, they were cut with slits called 'slashings', through which brilliantly coloured silk linings spilled out. For headgear, men wore velvet or brocade caps with a small brim.

Although women also wore ruffs, they favoured stiff lace collars that fanned up in the back like a frame around the head. German women, who dressed in a more conservative fashion than other European women, rejected the vertugado, ruff and double sleeves. Instead, they wore close-fitting caps and long pleated dresses of rich material with decorated bodices. Women in the Netherlands wore similar fashions, except that their caps, which were stretched on a small frame, were broader.

Clothes worn to play the game of real tennis

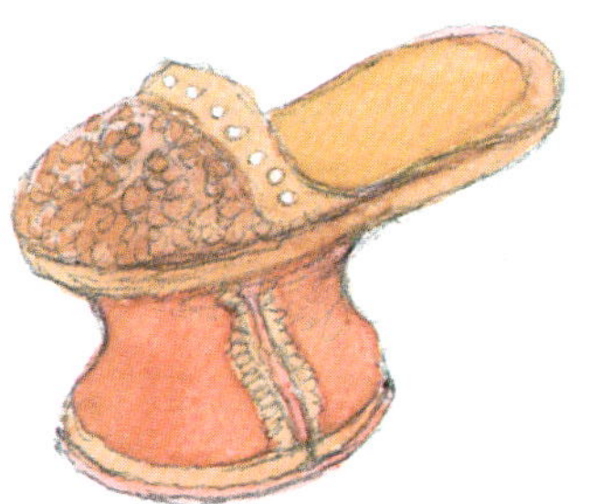

Clothes were stitched while on the person wearing them. Padding and skirts widened by metal hoops made the waists look smaller. Starched muslin ruffs became so large, that the handles of spoons had to be made longer so that people could reach their mouths!

Shoes, made of either soft leather or fine material, were comfortable. Venetian records mention shoes that were designed with heels almost 15 cm high, practical in Venice's high-tide floods perhaps.

European expansion overseas was a driving force in the 16th and 17th centuries. In just a few decades, Spain gained control of all of Central America and the Philippines; while by the mid-16th century, Portugal had some fifty trade and military bases on the African and Asian coasts. As France and England struggled over their possessions in North America during the 17th century, the Dutch East India Company became the most powerful European trading interest in the Orient.

For at least two centuries, the European countries that bordered the Atlantic battled over their overseas colonies, until finally, with the defeat of Holland and Spain, England won control of the high seas. With this kind of turmoil going on, it was necessary to expand both merchant and fighting fleets during these years.

Journeys across the Atlantic or around the Cape of Good Hope were long and difficult. The food was so poor that the shortage of vitamins often caused diseases such as scurvy. In addition to the perils of the sea itself, there was always the threat of attack by pirates or enemy ships, a danger that forced vessels to arm themselves with cannon, harquebuses (portable guns) and mortars.

Travelling by land was not much more comfortable. The earliest coaches were mounted on the axles of iron-ringed wheels with no suspension, so that even a short journey on the rough roads of the day was very uncomfortable. Not until the middle of the 16th century was the coach suspended on leather straps. Springs appeared much later. Despite improvements, frequent stops were necessary for the comfort of the passengers.

In mid-16th-century Paris, there were only three coaches, one for the queen, one for the king's mistress and one for a certain nobleman who was granted permission by the king to travel by carriage because he was too fat to ride a horse!

This cross-section of a small galleon shows the recently invented pump that removed water that collected in the ship's bilge. The large hold is filled with barrels of wet sand that served as ballast to stabilize the ship. On the top deck an officer takes a sighting with a sextant; below, in his cabin, the captain writes in his log-book; below the captain's cabin, the helmsman steers while a sailor stands ready to throw the plumb line (a lead-weighted line to measure the sea's depth).

The discovery of the new continents and the new understanding of the universe (based on the sun-centred theories of Copernicus, the founder of modern astronomy) stimulated the invention of new devices. These devices were to help research and measure physical, geographical and astronomical phenomena. Modern science, based on practical experimentation and statistical comparison, was born.

The mechanical clock was used in Europe in the 13th century. By the 17th century, the pendulum clock had been invented, based on principle discovered in the late 16th century by Galileo. Lenses, which had been used for glasses since the 13th century, were also improved. With the newly discovered telescope, Galileo not only discovered the moons of Jupiter, but also demonstrated Copernicus' theory about the *heliocentric* (Sun-centred) arrangement of the universe.

Leonardo da Vinci's civil and military engineering designs, including machines for human flight, anticipated many inventions that required more advanced technology than was available in his time (1452–1519).

Other less spectacular, although not necessarily less important, discoveries included analytic geometry, infinitesimal calculus and mathematical logic, which was essential for physics. Theory and application went hand in hand: the need to test new theories stimulated inventions and, in turn, more new theories.

The demands of warfare have always been an incentive for developing new technology. Improvements in iron technology made it possible to build cannon strong enough to withstand explosion. This allowed gunpowder, known since the Middle Ages, to be used in mortars. These new inventions in turn changed the way in which wars were fought.

The need for precise measurements of time in new areas of discovery helped the invention of clocks such as the three shown here.

A universal solar clock made in 17th-century Germany

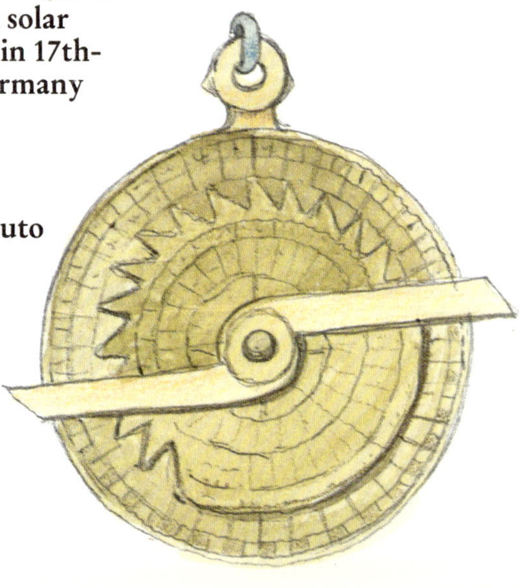

A clock made by Lorenzo di Bevenuto in Italy in 1511

A pendulum clock

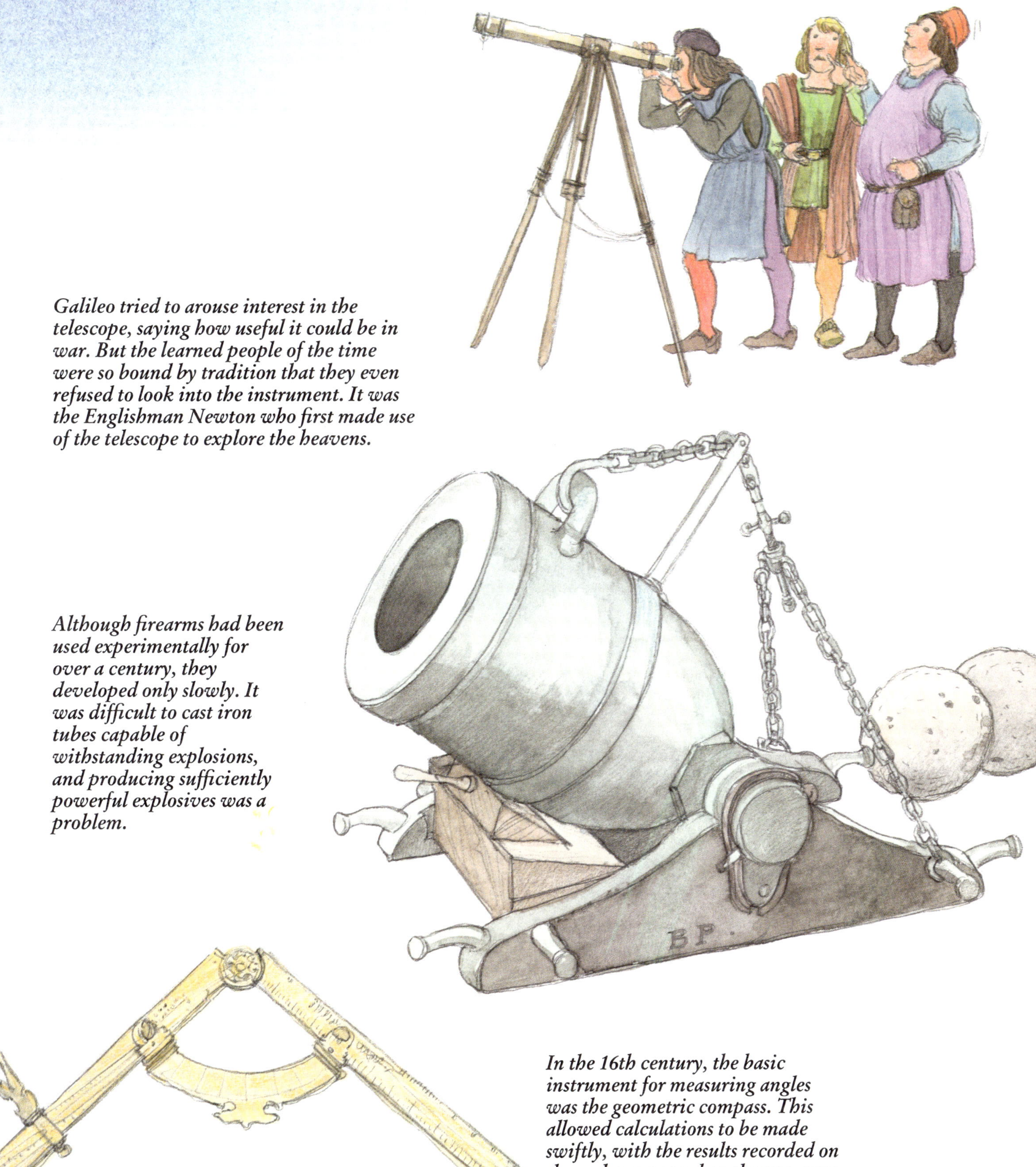

Galileo tried to arouse interest in the telescope, saying how useful it could be in war. But the learned people of the time were so bound by tradition that they even refused to look into the instrument. It was the Englishman Newton who first made use of the telescope to explore the heavens.

Although firearms had been used experimentally for over a century, they developed only slowly. It was difficult to cast iron tubes capable of withstanding explosions, and producing sufficiently powerful explosives was a problem.

In the 16th century, the basic instrument for measuring angles was the geometric compass. This allowed calculations to be made swiftly, with the results recorded on the scales engraved on the two arms of the compass.

95

Each European monarch's army, whether large or small, evolved into a permanent body (corps) which staged military parades, a new tradition that involved flags, drums, uniforms and brilliant displays of colour. Articulated plate armour or armour of tempered iron was common, as was the sallet helmet, which had a movable visor that protected the neck as well as the head.

In the 16th century, the two traditional army divisions of cavalry and infantry were joined by an equally important third division – artillery. Because the quality of a gun depended on its barrel and because its reliability depended on its firing mechanism, the first firearms were quite primitive. It was not until the invention of mechanical firing device that left a soldier's hands free, that the firearm became more effective.

Cannon fire was far more effective. Large stone cannon-balls, weighing up to a *quintel* (roughly 100 kilograms) tore huge holes in wooden ships and were equally damaging to the old walls of medieval towns and castles.

Italian plate armour

Mercenary commanders

A Spanish captain

**A German mercenary
(pikeman)**

Until smaller but more powerful iron cannon-balls replaced the old stone ones, heavy artillery, too cumbersome for campaigning, was used almost exclusively in sieges.

War professionals, the captain of the mercenaries (left) assembled companies of soldiers and offered their services to the highest bidder. In such mercenary armies the esprit de corps was always strong.

Milanese helmets

A Spanish arquebusier

The best Italian artillery came from Venice, with its famous falcons, muskets, arquebuses and cannon.

97

 # The Age of Revolution

In the 18th century the French monarchy preserved an 'absolutist' system. This allowed for a privileged class of non-producers such as the nobility and high-level clergy, but ignored the demands of the *bourgeoisie* (the middle class), which was the strongest economic force in society. The ideas of liberty and justice, put forward by 18th-century intellectuals and adopted by democratic groups, led directly to the overthrow of the old regime. Towards the end of the century, a violent revolution that began in July 1789, destroyed French monarchial absolutism once and for all. This sent winds of change throughout the rest of Europe.

A new military force, no longer made up of professional soldiers but drawn from the people, emerged after the French Revolution. Under Napoleon Bonaparte, this army won rapid and spectacular victories all across Europe, right into the heart of Russia.

Gilded ladies and gallant fops of the French aristocracy either paid for their idle and luxurious life-style under the guillotine, or fled the country over roads thick with soldiers of the French National Guard.

The common people, who were kept ignorant and illiterate, with no sense of their own rights, resigned themselves to their wretched conditions.

The landowning aristocracy fenced in the countryside and studied new methods of production.

Meanwhile, in England, monarchs had to answer to the law – more specifically to Parliament. King Charles I was executed in 1649 for forgetting this. After the civil war Parliament introduced a Bill of Rights. This bill established that the king and queen are considered to be 'first among equals'. In the House of Lords and the House of Commons, the two chambers of Parliament, all social and economic forces were represented – except the common people. The battle to give every adult the right to vote still lay in the future, but some people began to question the government's right to claim obedience from its citizens without granting them a say in how their country should be governed. Meanwhile, the spirit of independence, which lay at the heart of the English style of government, was flourishing far from home in the American colonies. With the American War of Independence (1775–1783), the United States of America came into being.

The mercantile and entrepreneurial middle classes protected their own interests. They did this by keeping the rights on colonial resources, and by making investments in industry.

New mines and urban factories came as a godsend to peasants who had been driven from the land and who desperately needed work.

As the various social classes emerged, so their different ways of life became apparent in their homes. A typical 18th-century aristocratic town house would have had suites of 'apartments': the kitchens and pantry were on the lower ground floor; reception rooms, where guests were received and formal meals eaten, on the ground floor; family living quarters on the next floor; above these, bedrooms; and finally, in the attic, servants' quarters. Although wood-burning fireplaces were built into every room, the newly invented ceramic or metal stove, fuelled by either wood or coal, was used occasionally. With lighting still provided by candles, elaborately carved wooden candleholders and crystal and ceramic chandeliers came into fashion.

There were no lavatories or bathrooms, and so refuse was disposed of outside on dungheaps or in cesspits. Running water was not available and water had to be carried into the house and left in jugs in the bedroom, or wherever it was needed.

With the widespread fencing-in of land, poor country people lost some of the rights that had helped them survive, such as being allowed to graze, hunt, fish and collect wood. Consequently, many of the poor drifted into the towns and cities where rapidly increasing industry was attracting labour. These working-class people lived in terraces of tiny houses packed close together, with two rooms downstairs and two bedrooms upstairs. The kitchen, which opened on to the street, became the main living room because it was the only warm room in the house.

The design of the English town house was adopted by the middle classes in American cities. The pioneers, who settled in the American wilderness, lived in primitive log cabins built with a fireplace in the centre. Guns were essential, as a defence against both wild animals and human marauders.

Mines, foundries and factories were surrounded by houses built by the factory owners for their workers. These houses were better than the tenements and slums that overpopulation in the towns and cities would bring later.

Aristocratic town house

Until the introduction of machinery, agriculture remained unchanged for centuries. Although new farming techniques evolved through scientific study and experimentation in the 18th century, old tools such as ploughs, harrows, rollers, scythes, forks and rakes continued to be made, and were improved.

In England, where there was political stability and where a population explosion produced many mouths to feed, agriculture changed radically. To obtain maximum yield from the land, fertilizers were developed, and crop rotation was studied so that better harvests could be produced without impoverishing the soil. The land-owning gentry and aristocracy lived close to the source of their wealth, their land. They took a direct interest in farming and tried out new ideas. The English people, especially farmers, enjoyed a comparatively healthy diet.This probably contributed to their population growth as well as to their longer lifespan.

Maize

Water mill

*New crops, such as tobacco, were
introduced into Europe from the colonies.
Maize, already brought into Europe from
Russia, was grown so widely that it became
a staple crop in some areas.*

*Coffee and tea from the East and cocoa
from the Americas became popular
beverages in Europe.*

Tobacco

Coffee

All sorts of water-powered and hand-powered machines were redesigned to be driven by steam, a step which revolutionized production. With looms, pumps, industrial hammers and even boats now working by steam, new work patterns were needed to make the most of this new source of energy.

Mechanization turned the skilled craftsman or artisan into an unskilled factory hand who had no direct contact with the finished product. Mechanization speeded up the production of goods, which meant that costs went down and the market broadened.

The main source of energy during the steam age was coal and more and more people were needed to work in the coal mines. Coal mining by faint lantern light deep underground was one of the toughest jobs of the day. With the persistent danger of collapsing shafts and flooding, as well as the threat of respiratory illness, suffocation and gas explosions, miners suffered for their livelihood. While large horses were still used for raising the mined coal up the shafts, tiny 'pit ponies', and women and children, worked down the pits, pulling small trucks along the narrow passageways. Engine-powered machines were not used in the mines until it was shown that they would be more profitable than employing humans alone.

Great quantities of coal were also used in the production of iron, a metal that was increasingly in demand both for weapons and various mechanical objects. Guns and steam engines both developed slowly; the manufacture of each requiring an iron cylinder that could withstand severe and prolonged stress. It was only with the advances in steel production that these strong materials appeared.

The main concern in the Industrial Revolution was productivity (producing as much as possible in as short a time as possible). And so, a strict check was kept on time during the working day. Sunrise, midday and sunset were no longer announced by bells, but by mechanical clocks with springs and cogs. A new breed of craftsman emerged, the clockmaker, whose trade demanded not only love of mechanisms, but a dedication to precision as well.

Coal mining

Horses were still
widely used for all
types of work, and so
the power of a
machine was measured
in terms of horsepower,
or what a horse could
accomplish.

With the discovery and conquest of new lands overseas, the Mediterranean lost its importance in international trade. Also, as ships began to load directly from the markets of India and the West Indies, the dangerous and expensive old caravan routes were gradually abandoned too. Countries bordering the Atlantic now competed for supremacy in international trade and fought sea battles for control of ports and markets. Old trade ports such as Venice lost their power for ever.

Before the industrialization of Europe, handmade goods from India and China were comparable in quality but much cheaper than those produced in Europe, while slave labour on the plantations of America made for very competitive prices.

The result of all these imports flooding the European markets was that merchants, through their financial strength, became the most powerful class in society.

At about the same time, paper money began to be printed. Money issued by the state no longer had to be in coinage of a certain weight of gold or silver. It might simply be a piece of paper to which the state gave a certain value. This value was in turn related to the reserves of gold in the national treasury.

The stock exchange was the place for those who enjoyed the risky business of speculating on the rise and fall of companies.

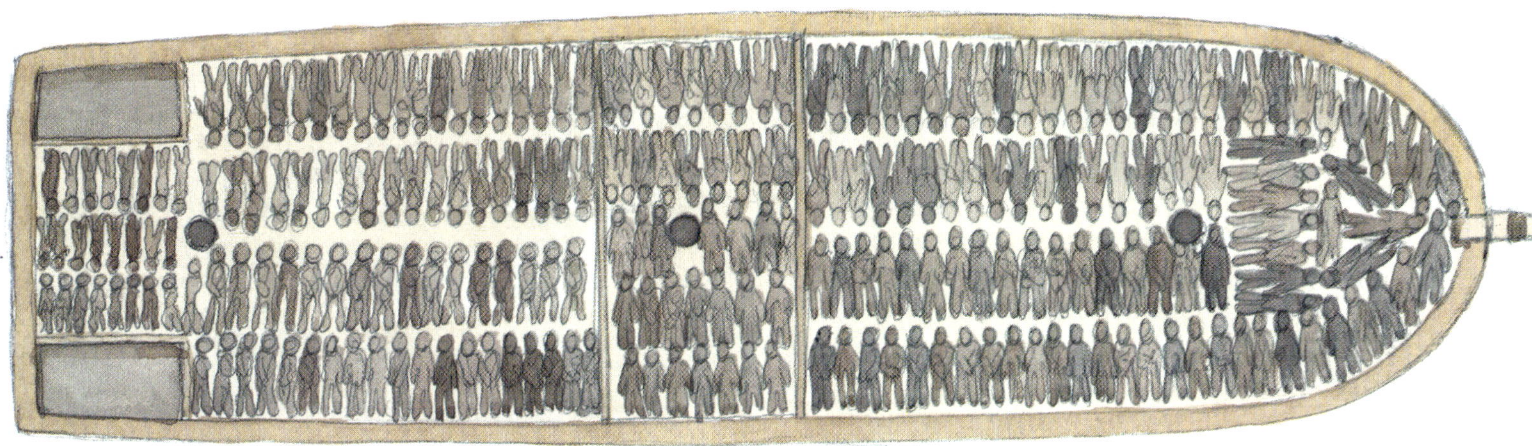

During the 18th century, some two million slaves were transported to British colonies alone. The ever-expanding cotton, coffee and cocoa plantations in the Americas required more and more slaves. The slave ship shown here indicates how many slaves were crammed into the hold for a journey of several months. About 20 per cent of them would die before the ship reached its destination.

Coffee

Cacao (cocoa)

107

Eighteenth-century materials, clothes and fashions were among the most elaborate in the history of fashion. Silk was the most popular material.

Until the revolution, women in France continued to wear artificially widened skirts that were stretched out over a basket structure of three hoops, with the top hoop painfully pulling in the waist. Because such skirts were not functional to wear, the hoops became more oval and wider at the sides so that their wearers could at least pass through doorways or climb into coaches sideways. The hair-styles were elaborate with hair often heavily powdered, but the fashion changed when Queen Marie-Antoinette set a trend for a natural hair style.

English women wore less elaborate clothes: a short jacket pushed out at the back by a bustle under the skirt, a tight bodice and a full, although not hooped, skirt were common.

Men wore silk stockings, breeches, shirts tied at the collar with a scarf, a waistcoat and a light overcoat. The waistcoat sometimes extended down to the knee, while the overcoat, no more than a long jacket, was tight across the chest, wide at the bottom and slit up the back.

With the start of the French Revolution (1789–1793), silks and brocades were replaced by the 'democratic' dress of the common people. Shops selling reasonably priced ready-made clothes first appeared in Paris, then the capital of fashion.

Although the middle classes followed
aristocratic fashions, they did not indulge
in the lavish materials and flamboyant
hair-styles of the rich, even when they
could afford it. Indeed, the huge wigs and
powdered pigtails gathered in a bow at the
back of the neck and worn by men, were
criticized for being reactionary.
Except for their bright colours and braid,
military uniforms were similar to the
clothes of the middle class men. Now, boots,
which had been common in the 17th
century, were no longer convenient for
civilian use and were replaced by low court
shoes with buckles. Women's shoes,
decorated with delicate embroidery,
became increasingly elegant.

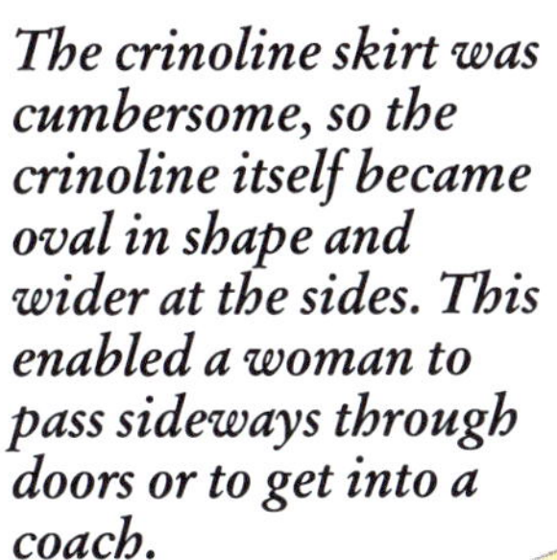

The crinoline skirt was
cumbersome, so the
crinoline itself became
oval in shape and
wider at the sides. This
enabled a woman to
pass sideways through
doors or to get into a
coach.

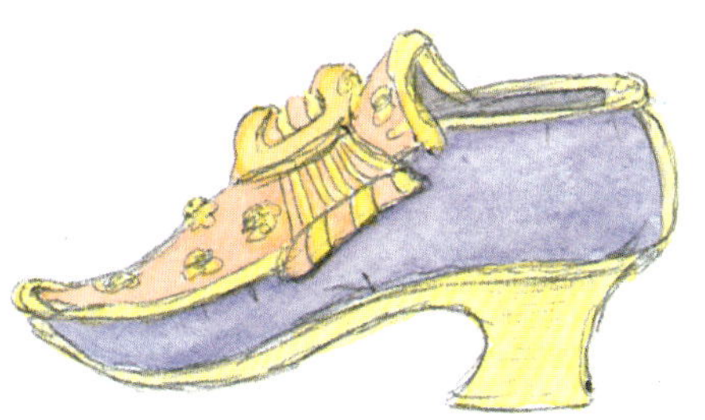

In the 18th century, the design of wooden sailing ships came near to perfection. Although the armed vessels of the British East India Company were the finest ships afloat, there were a few noticeable differences between the ships of the various European countries. Around 1700, the helm became a wheel rather than a tiller, which made steering more precise and lessened the risk of losing control during sudden gusts of wind. The best known of all the English ships in service during the 18th century was the *Victory*, which mounted 102 cannons and sailed with a crew of 850. It was from this ship that Admiral Horatio Nelson directed the defeat of Napoleon's Franco-Spanish fleet at Trafalgar in 1805.

Roads were still bad. Travellers could go only a few kilometres a day at most and transporting goods overland greatly increased the final cost. The need for improvements led to studies and experiments that eventually brought about changes in modern road-building techniques. France built a network of major roads that all converged on Paris, while other European countries undertook similar projects. To finance the construction and maintenance of roads, England revived the toll system whereby travellers had to pay in order to pass through gates at certain points along the road. The new and improved roads helped to establish an efficient postal service as well as a passenger service that used comfortable, sprung coaches. But a long journey was still an adventure – and not always a pleasant one.

Early experimental private steam vehicles also ventured out on the new roads, but they were charged such high tolls that the experiments were soon abandoned; they were not resumed until decades later, on a different type of road – the railway.

Sailing ships which braved crossing oceans carried a spread of sails which made the vessels easier to handle and safer in all conditions.

On the new network of roads a regular public transport service came into being.

At the end of the 18th century, man came close to achieving one of his most ancient desires, to fly. The first passengers rose up in a 'boat' suspended from a balloon and hovered in the air above Paris for more than 20 minutes.

Among the first steam-powered vehicles was Nicolas Joseph Cugnot's road wagon of 1769; it ran at nearly five kilometres an hour and could carry four passengers. Unfortunately, Cugnot did not seem to have much interest in brakes. During a test drive, the vehicle hit a wall and was damaged beyond repair!

The steam engine, which heralded the beginning of the Industrial Revolution, was undoubtedly the most important invention of the 18th century. At last, people had a means of converting heat energy into mechanical energy, a supply of energy that was not dependent on wind or water as mills had been. Steam engines could be transported to places where they were needed and used fuel such as coal, that was readily available. Water was heated in a cylinder to create a head of steam pressure. This in turn pushed a movable element within the cylinder, releasing energy that could run all kinds of machines.

Equally important for industry were the advances in chemistry: a better understanding of the structure of matter and of the laws governing the structure of elements in different substances was achieved. Chemistry involved the observation of the various processes that matter undergoes. Such observations enabled chemists to reproduce these processes in order to create a variety of products such as dyes, solvents, fertilizers and detergents.

One indirect result of this chemical research was the discovery of a new form of energy – electricity. Although electricity was familiar as a natural phenomenon, it was not until the invention of batteries that it could at last be harnessed. Early batteries consisted of a number of alternating copper and zinc sheets with an acid solution between them. The resulting movement of electrons from one pole of the battery to the other produced an electrical charge.

In the field of optics, microscopes, which for the first time revealed a world of micro-organisms in an ordinary drop of water or blood, were developed. Medicine could at last begin its fight against infectious diseases.

The hydraulic pump, known as 'the miner's friend', was powered by a steam engine. The piston movement, transmitted to the arm of the pump, pumped water out of mines continuously.

A coach with springs for a more comfortable ride.

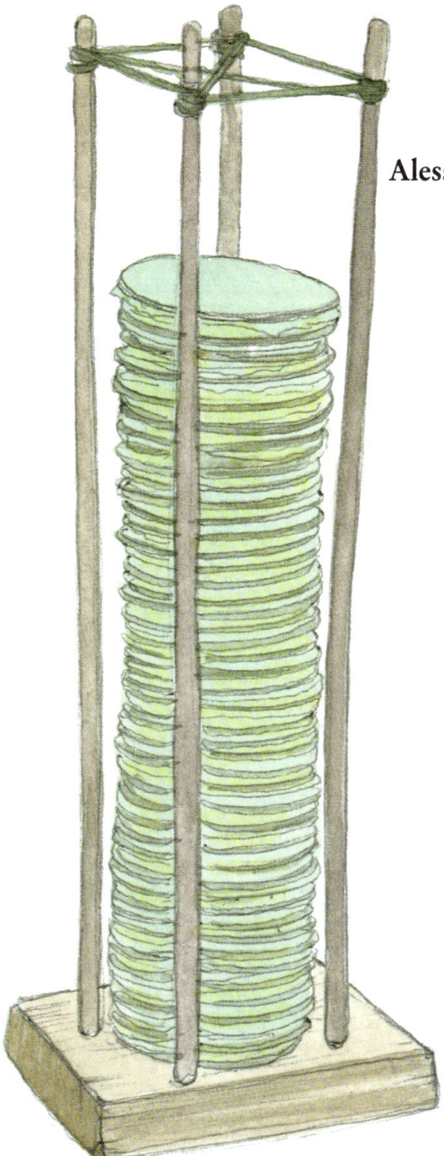

Alessandro Volta's battery (1800)

Robert Hooke's microscope (17th century)

Bearings and suspension made coach travel comfortable. The process of mechanization became a game. The mechanical duck below, complete with its own digestive system, is a good example of a mechanized toy.

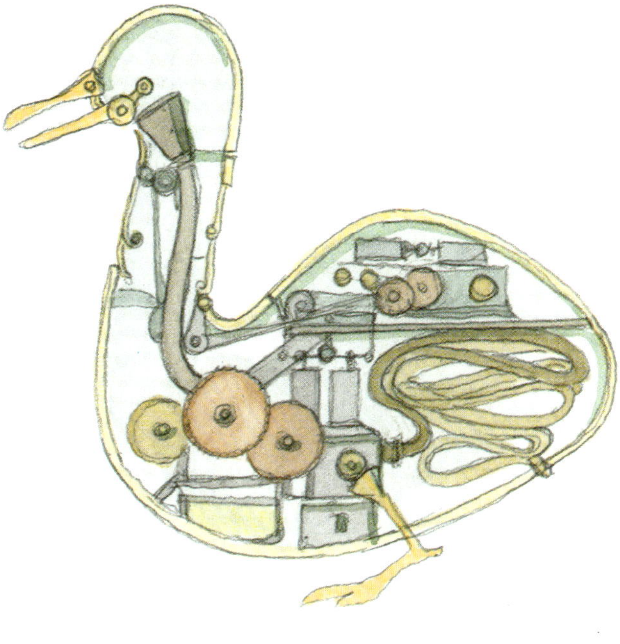

The 18th century began with the War of the Spanish Succession (1701–1713) and ended with the early Napoleonic campaigns. Bitter wars were also fought over the succession to the Polish and Austrian thrones during the 18th century. It was a period in which Europe's armies remained in constant active service.

As firearms became more effective, new tactical thinking was needed in warfare. The cavalry temporarily lost its importance, at least until rear-loading guns and pistols with automatic firing mechanisms were invented. Heavy cannons were now only mounted on ships. On land, the more manoeuvrable models with more accurate sightings were used to zoom in on specific targets rather than batter holes in walls. Battle lines were still drawn up close together so that bullets continued to inflict damage.

All the great European armies introduced an elite cavalry corps of hussars. These were fighting men who, like the original hussar corps of Hungary, were held in awe for their bravery and ruthlessness in action. *Sabreurs*, cavalrymen who carried curved swords called sabres, favoured surprise charges. They often proved to be the decisive factor in a battle.

A French drummer and musketeer

Prussian artillery

A field cannon

114

Prussian grenadiers wearing typical headgear, similar to that of the British grenadiers

In Prussia, under Frederick II, the tallest and strongest soldiers were selected to become grenadiers, so named because they were armed with hand grenades. The grenadier first lit the fuse of the gunpowder-packed grenade and then hurled it into the distance, where it would explode. Such hand grenades fell into disuse, but they have been used again in more recent wars.

In hussar regiments, a man and his horse formed an inseparable unit. The hussars wore an 'international' uniform that was, with minor variations, the same in all armies. The fur jerkin, slung over the left shoulder, acted as a shield for the least protected part of the body.

The Age of Progress

The major powers of Europe came together at the Congress of Vienna in 1815 in an effort to restore stability among the European states. They attempted to prevent the defeated Napoleon from having any more influence. They also tried to wipe out the memory of the French Revolution. However, under the pressure of liberal ideas, nearly all 19th-century European monarchs had to accept that freely elected representatives of the society would participate in government. Not only did the Liberals fight to bring about unified nations whose people shared a common background, but they also fought for freedom.

In this century Italy and Germany both became united countries, Greece shook off Ottoman (Turkish) domination and Czechs and Poles formed independent nations. Small but active groups developed more advanced ideas about republican and democratic forms of government, egalitarian and communist societies, and even anarchy.

Following Great Britain's lead in industrial developments, the rest of Europe and the United States rapidly turned to mechanized means of production. With an almost unlimited faith in the possibilities of technological progress, investors poured capital earned by agriculture and colonial trade, into industry.

Urbanization – the shift of population from the country to the cities and towns – was another phenomenon that took place in nearly every country. Industrialized cities grew rapidly; their skylines, once dominated by cathedrals and government buildings, now bristled with factory chimneys. In France it was estimated that for every ten people living in the country, one lived in town. While in Britain, where industrialization had started fifty years earlier, the proportion of urban dwellers was twice as high.

Another factor in this shift of population was the new and rapid means of transport – the railways.

Constitutional monarchy

The moral authority of the clergy

The legislative and judiciary power of parliament and the magistrature

The national army

The enterprising middle classes

The ideological revolutionary

At first the working classes objected to being herded together in the factories and down the mines, and they protested against mechanization. In the end, they had to accept the harsh discipline of working under the difficult conditions.

In the mid-18th century people could travel only a few kilometres a day, by the mid-19th century, trains were already reaching about 40 kilometres an hour, although there was very little track. This new means of transport meant faster delivery of goods and information, not to mention passengers.

117

During this industrial revolution, major cities in northern Europe and the United States changed dramatically. Industrial zones and the new residential areas sprawled around the old city centres, and railway stations were linked to the old quarters by broad avenues. To avoid overcrowding and because of lack of facilities in the older areas of cities, whole districts were demolished and rebuilt.

Public hygiene became important. Complex sewage systems were constructed, drinking water was piped directly to houses through lead, and later, steel pipes, and cemeteries were built outside the cities. The most ambitious example of urban change in the 19th century was the design and building of the great boulevards in Paris.

The main architectural style was *neo-classicism*, seen in the huge, impressive residential blocks of the time. Towards the end of the 19th century, a more decorative style, *art nouveau*, appeared. At the same time, the building trade introduced new techniques for using steel and reinforced concrete.

The middle-class private house was large and functional, well heated, well lit and easy to clean. Economical white-enamelled iron stoves with a chimney tube for the smoke and a hood to catch the steam were placed in the old fireplaces. Iceboxes replaced smelly larders, while adjustable oil lamps provided light, copper tubs and a boiler heated water in the newest room in the house – the bathroom.

The gap between rich and poor was clearly demonstrated by the difference in their living conditions. Working classes, lived in old, tumbledown houses that backed on to the new avenues, or in smoke-clogged suburbs around the factories. The miserable living conditions of the workers became a chief concern of philanthropists, reformers and enlightened politicians, notably the Socialists.

Country families, small landowners and tenants alike, lived in houses that had changed little over centuries. There was a kitchen, where most activities took place, and a bedroom where parents and children slept together. In a stable, either under the house or next to it, the animals were kept.

The inside of a town house.
Main streets were lit by gas
lamps tended by a
lamplighter. People could now
walk about safely outside at
night. Roadsweepers kept the
streets clean, and now that it
was possible to hire cabs and
use public transport, it was no
longer necessary to own a
coach and horses.

Improvements in farming developed in the Netherlands and Britain and spread throughout Europe. They were important not only to landowners and those who worked on the land, but to the state as well. The sweeping changes in land ownership in France that followed the Revolution helped both agriculture and the farmer, and the Napoleonic wars destroyed for ever the system of glebe peasantry (where land and its revenue belonged to the Church).

Although serfdom was abolished in 1861 in Russia, farming communities remained in a state of semi-serfdom. Meanwhile, in the United States, slavery continued on large plantations in the South and was not abolished until 1865.

Mechanization drew many workers from the land, as the new farm machinery either shortened the hours on a job or did away with the job altogether. On the vast farms of America, huge, new steam-powered threshing machines attached to early mechanical harvesters did the work of many people.

Advances in chemistry improved methods of treating and preserving food. Sugar could now be extracted from sugar-beet and this crop was grown almost everywhere.

Far from the stress of urban life, with only his own resources to rely on, the American farmer laboured to achieve something permanent for himself and his family. Striving for personal freedom in a new land often meant starting from scratch under difficult circumstances.

The first canned food

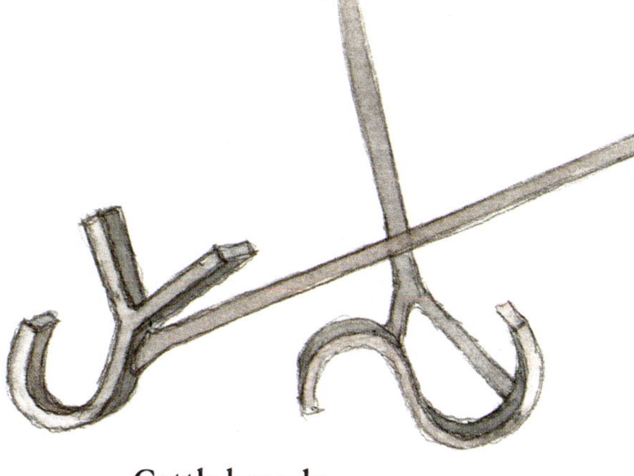

Cattle brands

Endless horizons opened up for the pioneer settlers in the American West; vast tracts of land were theirs to tame and cultivate. Cowboys, led a hard and lonely life, watching over and driving their herds of cattle.

Although new investment in equipment was constantly needed to keep up with the latest technology, industry proved to be highly profitable from the very beginning. Consequently, new production methods spread rapidly in northern Europe and the United States. While in more depressed areas, such as Italy, industrialization did not really get under way until the 20th century.

Despite the widespread use of steam power, human labour was still the major form of energy in the factories that continued to spring up in industrial cities. The new ideas of 'progress' dictated that production should improve all the time, that competitors should be defeated and markets captured. Most important was the urge to make profits that controlled production. Those who had to sweat and toil to produce wealth for others felt exploited. To protect their rights these workers began to organize themselves into *trade unions*.

There was little dignity attached to production-line work – people no longer had to master a trade, learn the secrets of a skill or become specialists in their craft. Even when the job required some thought, the worker had no sense of pride or achievement in the end product because he or she was never rewarded for the work done.

Because handmade goods produced with care to individual specifications were still valued, the traditional artisan had not vanished entirely. But since few people could afford such luxuries, the number of professional craftsmen continued to fall. In an attempt to recover some of the traditional values in the face of large-scale industry, William Morris started the Arts and Crafts movement in 19th-century Britain. Selecting and exhibiting work and designs in the applied arts – his wallpaper designs are particularly famous – he greatly influenced subsequent notions of taste.

Depending on the quality of carbon in iron, it can be soft iron or cast iron or it can be made into steel. Steel, the most flexible mixture of iron and carbon, is the best kind to use for sheeting; cast iron is hard but fragile; soft iron, although very malleable, weakens quickly. Special blast furnaces were designed to extract carbon from iron; above we see a huge steam-powered hammer for working steel.

Because some of the wealth from increased production went to finance new roads and railways (left), canals and irrigation systems and new public (administration) buildings, industrial progress also benefited the public. Such projects took years to complete and employed large numbers of workers.

These children (right) are not going to school, but to work in a factory or a mine.

Mechanization enabled European-produced goods to compete with those produced in the colonies although the colonies still supplied raw materials for European industry. Commerce in exotic goods was still a thriving business. Coffee and cocoa became increasingly popular.

It took generations for sailors to adopt mechanization. Shipyards also found it hard to change over to steam-powered ships still in their infancy in the 19th century. Sailing ships, with metal hulls and masts, tapering forms, huge sails and sophisticated rigging devices could stay at sea for long stretches of time under all sorts of conditions.

In the hope of making their fortunes, many people travelled to the remotest areas of the American continent to find gold. These gold prospectors were the vanguard of a great migration which, in a few decades, had settled in areas of the United States stretching from the Appalachian Mountains in the east to the Rockies and from there to the Pacific in the west. This expanding nation not only developed a vast independent trade base, but also quickly became competitive with Europe. By the end of the 19th century the United States had become the world's first fully industrialized nation.

Outside powers still had quite considerable control in Latin America. Although the major Latin American countries had attained formal independence, their resources were exploited to such a degree that any industrial or commercial growth they might have developed on their own was seriously undermined.

Gold prospectors

Tea was an important, widely used commodity, which made large profits for its importers.

From the very beginning, the United States had a sound economic structure. This was headed by imaginative managers and 'entrepreneurs' who welcomed new technology and were far-sighted in their investments. The Americans were motivated by a sense of great loyalty to their young country and by a feeling of breaking new frontiers.

Raw cotton from the United States was exported to Europe, where newly mechanized spinning and weaving factories made it into cloth.

The most perfect sailing ship ever designed was the very fast American clipper.

The tailors and dressmakers who had enjoyed aristocratic patronage before the French Revolution were now designing new styles for the newly-rich middle class.

Narrow waists returned, with billowing skirts concealing layers of petticoats. These petticoats were soon replaced by the *crinoline*, a stiffened underskirt of horsehair or stiff cotton, over which the full, light-textured skirt was stretched. Next came the half-crinoline, which puffed out only the lower part of the skirt. The material at the top of the skirt was gathered over padding at the small of the back so that the skirt hung down in broad swathes.

Men's fashions took their lead from England, where Beau Brummel, perhaps the greatest 'dandy' of the age, defined elegance as perfect dress sense. Being elegant meant being able to dress so appropriately for any function that one would not be noticed. Breeches, which were usually a different colour and material from the jacket, became longer and were buttoned down the front rather than at the sides. Until the appearance of the tailcoat, which was cut away at the waist with the tail flaps hanging behind, jackets were quite long. Wigs went completely out of fashion and hair was now worn very short, although shoulder-length hair was still acceptable. It was normal to wear a top hat. Shirts with upturned collars were worn with cravats of fine materials which were knotted and bowed in various styles.

For women, dressing was an elaborate, time-consuming business. Preparing for a reception or a ball usually required the help of at least one maid. The style of dress depended on the occasion; a cape was worn over the dress for shopping, a broad-collared dress and shawl was worn in the afternoon and evening wear was decolleté – low-necked to reveal neck and shoulders.

127

Enormous improvements in transport took place during the age of coal and steel. One of the major improvements was the development of steam-powered ships and trains in about the middle of the 19th century. Although the early iron ships built at the beginning of the century had been replaced by steel liners, the use of steam as a means of propulsion still presented problems. Naval engineers concentrated throughout the 19th century on the possibilities of either using paddle-wheels or propellers. Experiments proved that propellers completely immersed in the water provided the most efficient means of powered propulsion.

Iron rails had already been used successfully in the mines, where they replaced the old wooden tracks. They also proved to be hard-wearing when installed in city streets for horse-drawn trams. But the disadvantage was that the trams could only travel along set tracks.

The first locomotive to pull a passenger train, the *Catch-me-who-can*, little more than a demonstration model, appeared in 1808. One of the world's earliest public railways, the Liverpool-Manchester line, opened in 1830. It was the first railway line to rely completely on locomotive power. Within decades, rail networks were built everywhere and it became fashionable to use rail travel for holidays. Coach travel was left for those places that the railways had not yet reached. By the end of the century, steam locomotives had already begun to be replaced by diesel-electric locomotives. By the next century, the diesel-electric trains would in turn be replaced in many places by all-electric locomotives.

A transatlantic paddle steamer

A steam locomotive

The German inventor Otto Lilienthal, who successfully flew in a heavier-than-air machine, might be considered the true pioneer of modern flying. He built a series of flying machines, both monoplanes and biplanes, as well as gliders designed to be launched from hilltops. Lilienthal made over a thousand flights before a final fatal one in 1896.

Horse drawn tram

A stage coach

Steam was used more and more successfully but towards the end of the 19th century a new internal-combustion engine was developed which did not need a stock of coal or a cumbersome boiler. Instead, energy was produced by a piston in a cylinder, which was pushed by an explosion of air and combustible gas that was ignited by a spark. Later, for greater power, the mixture of air and fuel vapour was made to explode when compressed by the piston after it had sucked the mixture in. This engine was called a four-stroke engine because it worked in four main stages: induction, compression, ignition and exhaust. Petroleum became the main fuel.

The petrol engine was not only more efficient, but it could also be used in small private vehicles. Since the invention of bicycles had shown how much people enjoyed moving about freely by mechanical means, the later transition to motorcycles and automobiles was rapid.

Now that the old problem of rear loading was solved, progress was also made with firearms. With the invention of a movable mechanism that allowed the bullet charge to be set in place at the back of the barrel and a firing device that automatically set off the charge, ramrods, wadding and fuses were no longer necessary.

Electric batteries, which provided a continuous current were the impetus for many inventions, most notably the telegraph and the light bulb. The telegraph worked by using the electromagnetic effects of electrical current. Other properties of electrical current were used in the arc light and then in the filament light bulb.

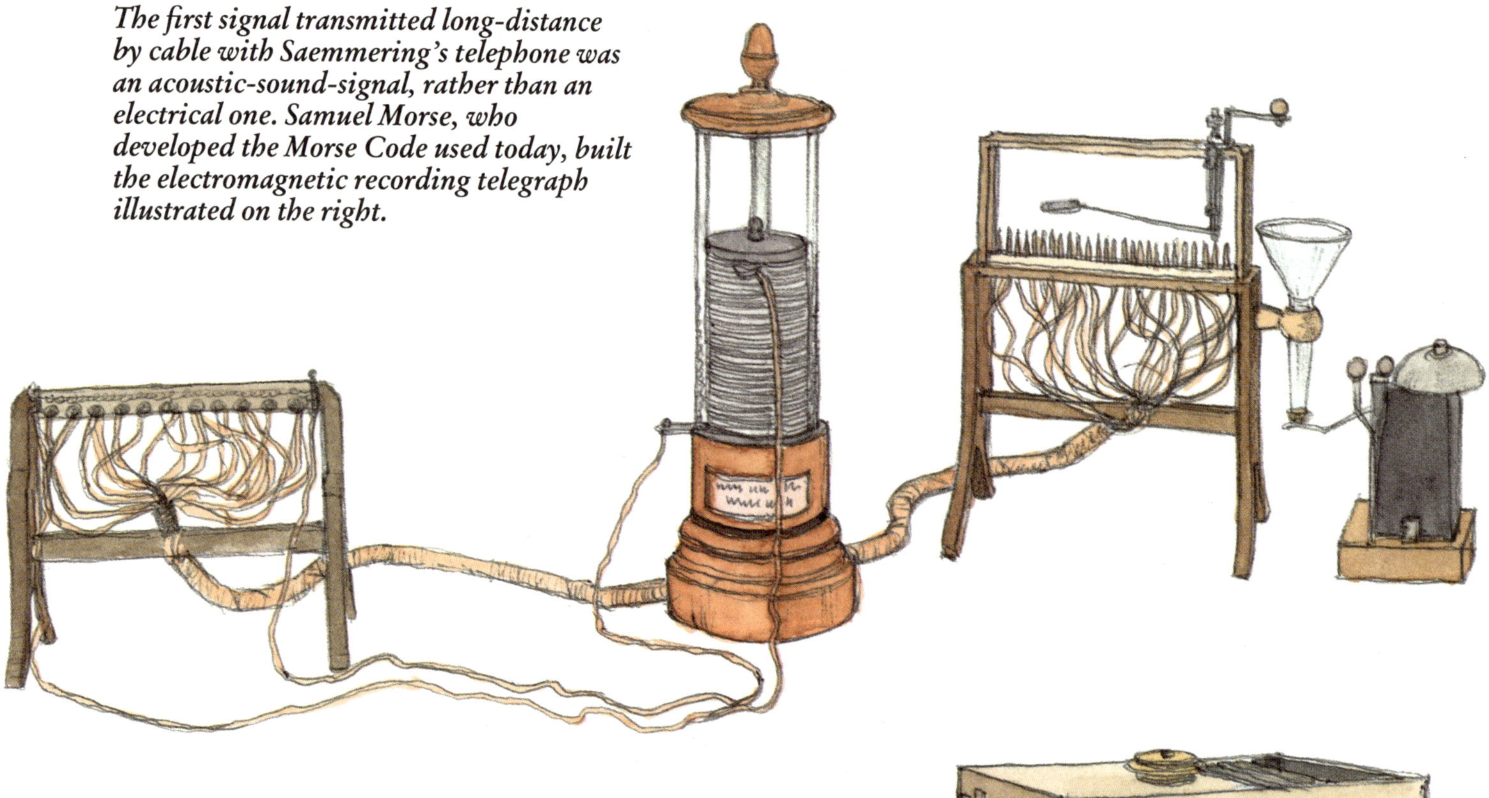

The first signal transmitted long-distance by cable with Saemmering's telephone was an acoustic-sound-signal, rather than an electrical one. Samuel Morse, who developed the Morse Code used today, built the electromagnetic recording telegraph illustrated on the right.

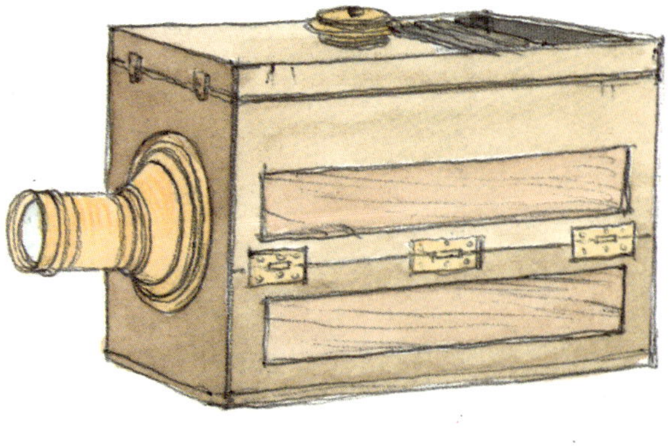

The earliest form of camera produced pictures by means of a glass plate covered with light-sensitive silver salts.

George Stephenson's steam locomotive first demonstrated the potential of railways, a form of transport that spread rapidly throughout 19th-century Europe.

Colt, Remington and Smith and Wesson were famous names everywhere. These American revolvers and rifles were the first automatic weapons with rotating bullet chambers.

By 1866 America and Europe were already linked by underwater telegraph cables.

For over twenty years after the French Revolution, the European states joined forces to combat the military genius of Napoleon, whose successful campaigns took him to the very heart of Russia. Welcomed and admired by the democrats of the countries he invaded, he soon began to show a thirst for power that Austria, Britain and Prussia were determined to keep in check.

In some of the most celebrated battles in history, Napoleon's armies won victories in Italy and Germany, but experienced suffering during the midwinter retreat from Russia and bitter defeat at Liepzig and Waterloo.

Napoleon's army was well armed, equipped and disciplined and each soldier carried his own cartridges of gunpowder and shot. Military ceremony, with all its pomp and formality, began with Napoleon.

For centuries, serious wounds on the battlefield were 'treated' by amputation, also known as the *coup de grace* or the 'mercy stroke'. In Napoleon's time, 'ambulance' wagons for carrying the wounded quickly to a field hospital accompanied the armies.

Napoleonic troops

Guns had bayonets fixed on the end for use both at a distance and at close quarters, providing the soldier with a two-in-one weapon. This picture shows 19th-century infantrymen and officers.

An ambulance

The infantry of the anti-Napoleonic coalition

Cartridge case, shot and cartridges

French grenadiers

The English infantry

133

# The Turn of the Century

Two major trends are important in helping us understand 20th-century prosperity: the concentration of the population in cities and the distribution of the work force in agriculture, industry and trade, and public services.

With the exception of ancient Rome, no European city had more than half a million inhabitants before 1750, and only two, London and Paris, had over half a million.

The shift of population from the countryside to towns, that is the shift from manual labour to mechanized labour, meant that less manpower was required to feed everybody. Even though the population was growing, increased productivity of the land and mechanization of labour enabled a smaller number of people to produce a greater quantity of food. Those workers no longer required to produce food turned to other employment. This in turn increased overall national productivity and prosperity.

At one time, farm workers formed the bulk of the work-force; other areas of the economy, no matter how important, employed far fewer people. This situation changed dramatically with the Industrial Revolution and the urbanization that followed. At the beginning of this century, about half the active population of industrialized countries worked the land. Their numbers have dropped steadily ever since.

In contrast, the number of workers in industry has only recently begun to level out. In fact, the percentage of industrial workers has begun to fall as industry can no longer support large numbers of employees. In the area of trade and public service, there has been an enormous upswing. The numbers of people employed in clerical, technical, managerial and academic jobs not directly concerned with production exceeds that of people in industry, and this gap continues to widen.

RUSSIA

One person in twenty lived in cities

Industry

Commerce and services

Agriculture

FRANCE

Two people in twenty lived in cities

Industry

Commerce and services

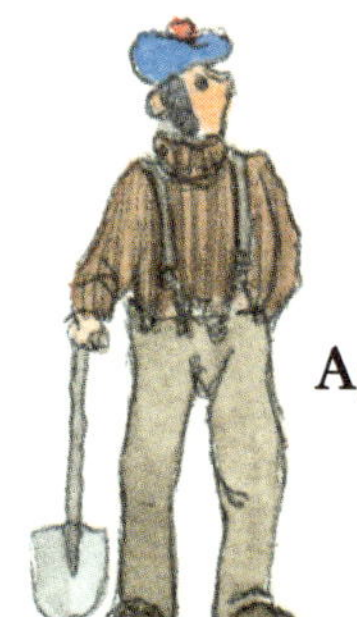

Agriculture

In the second half of the 19th century, urbanization spread.

GREAT BRITAIN
Four people in twenty lived in cities
Industry
Commerce and services
Agriculture
UNITED STATES
Five people in twenty lived in cities
Industry
Commerce and services
Agriculture

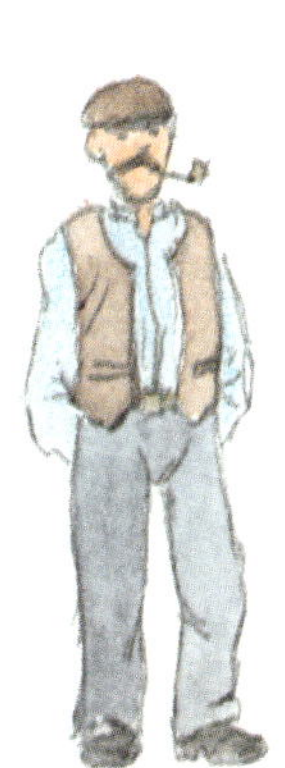

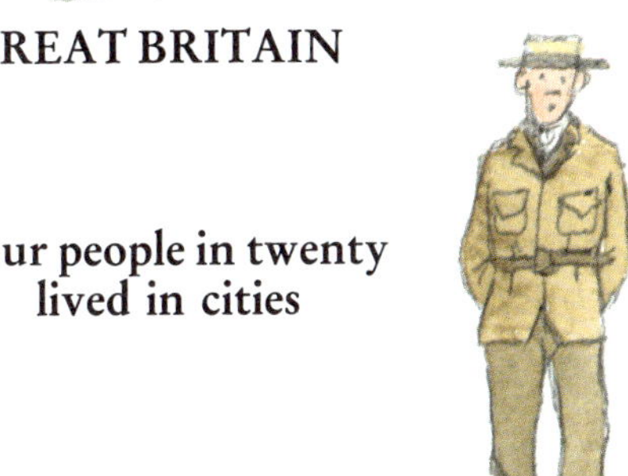

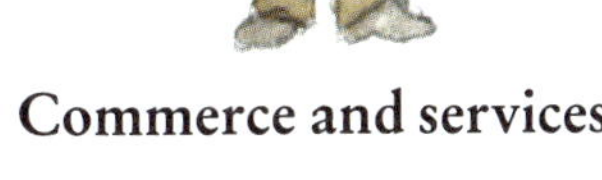

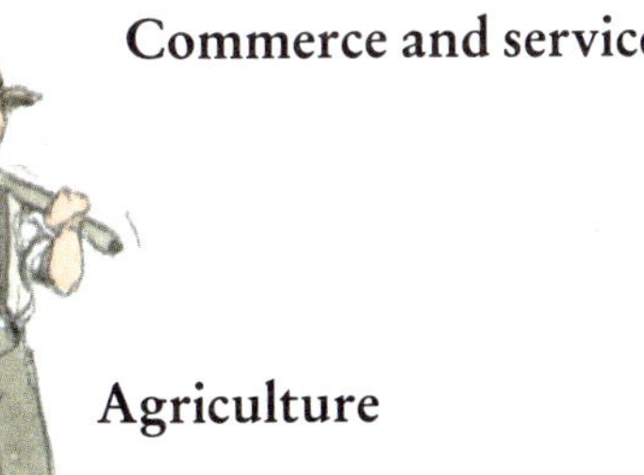

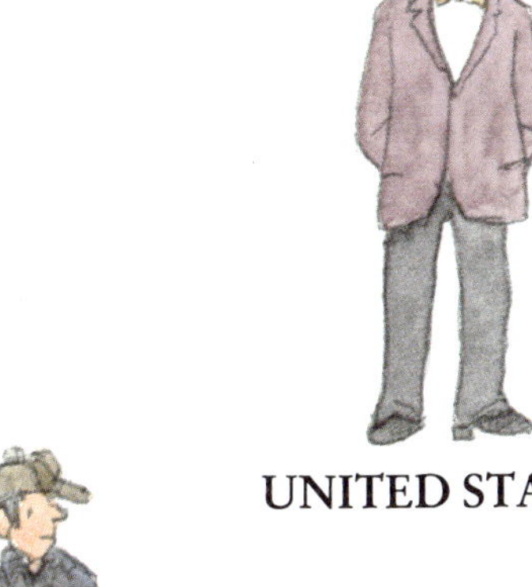

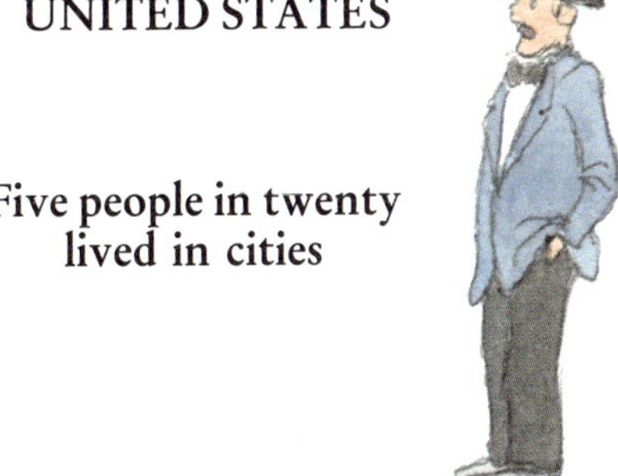

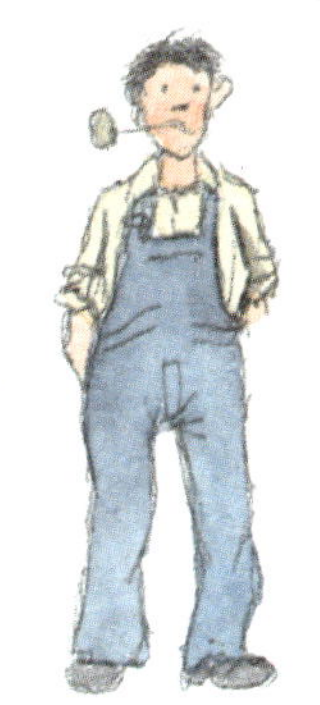

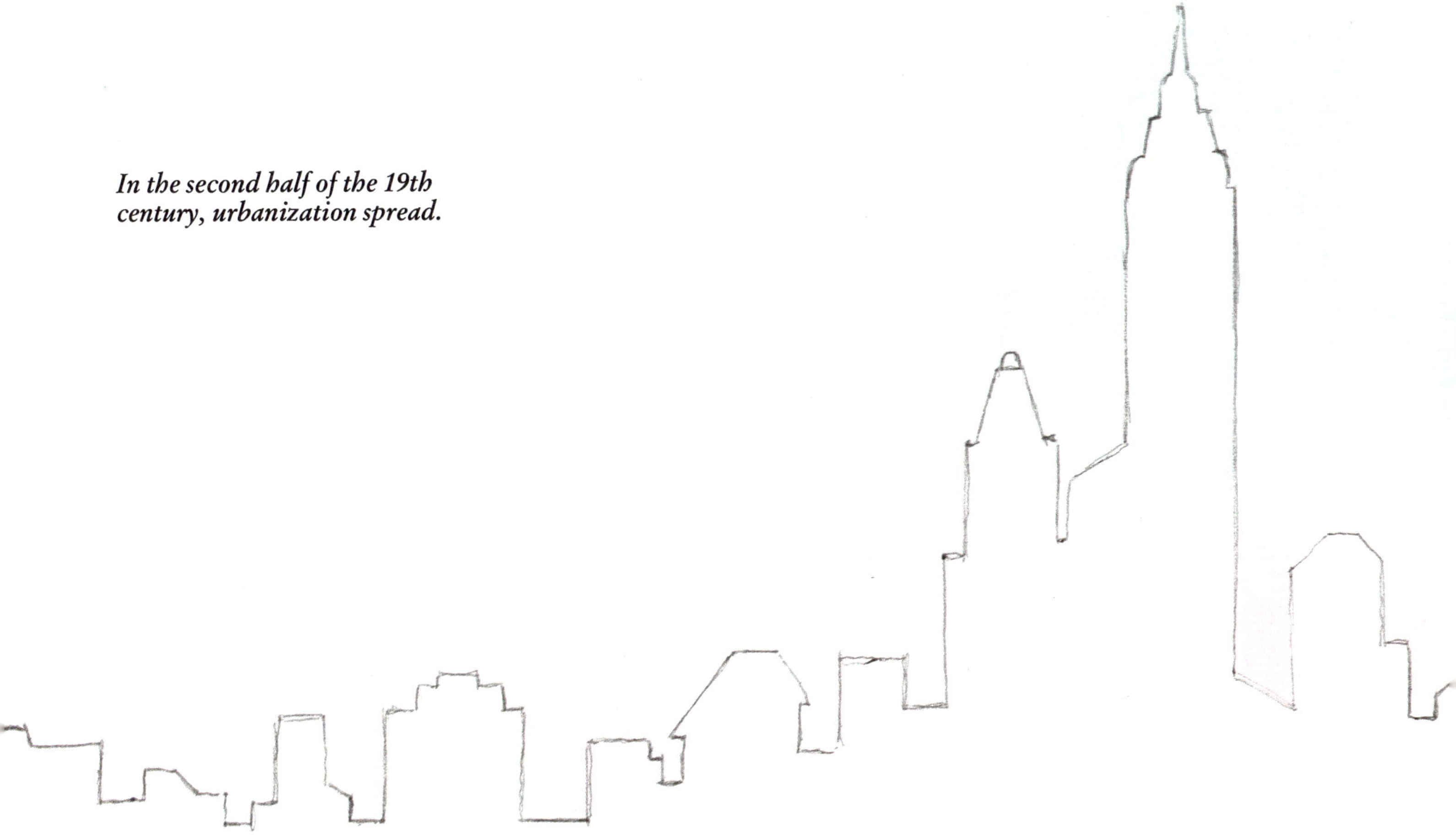

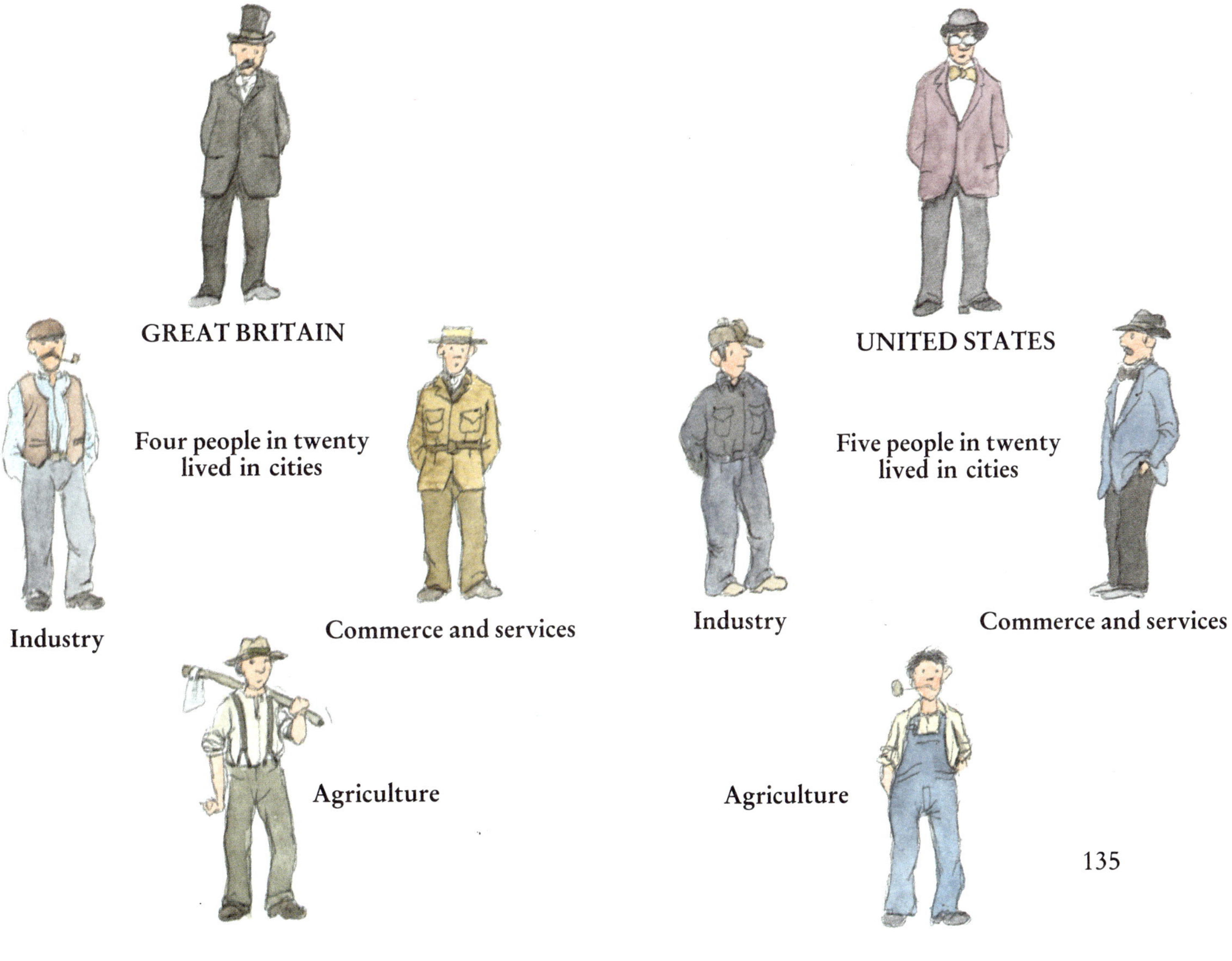

New building materials, including steel and reinforced concrete, opened up many opportunities for architects and engineers at the end of the 19th century. After World War I (1914–1918) in both Europe and America, functional design became the order of the day. The trend was to get away from traditional styles, to free the imagination in the search for new forms, and to make the most of the technological possibilities of new building materials.

Even in the most futuristic skyscraper, living space was planned according to everyday family needs, with no space going unused. Every dwelling had features that were pre-viously unknown – electric lights, gas, central heating, a refrigerator, bathrooms with hot and cold running water and all sorts of labour-saving electrical devices, such as vacuum cleaners and washing machines. Home communications changed greatly with the introduction of the telephone, radio and television.

Both the production of modern domestic appliances and the administration and mainten-ance of a modern city needs a huge workforce. Think of what lies below the streets of London or New York, or imagine just how much technology is needed to provide the necessary services to just one small town.

During World War I, a war that changed traditional ways once and for all, the most gifted European and American architects were already sketching out the shapes of the future. Furniture, now mass-produced, also became simpler and more functional, although designers retained a fondness for good materials and personal touches.

**Einstein Tower,
Potsdam, Germany, 1919**

New home comforts

The Empire State Building was built between 1930 and 1932. Its 381 metres made it for a long time the tallest building in the world.

Modern agriculture with its maximum productivity and mechanization of farming techniques, has seen its work-force dwindle over the years. In order to produce more food for less cost, farmers have cultivated the most fertile areas and abandoned less productive ones where for centuries peasants made their living. Research into fertilizers and irrigation techniques has increased output by as much as tenfold.

Neglect of mountain areas created serious problems. The hilly land around the Mediterranean, ideal for grape-vines and olive trees, has had to be carefully cultivated to make the most practical use of machinery.

On more level ground, ploughing with tractors has allowed maximum use of the top layer of soil. The tractors, used for many different jobs – pulling, pumping water from wells, driving other machines such as a thresher – is just one kind of agricultural machine that has been developed to make farm work easier and faster.

Nitrogen- and potassium-based fertilizers are used to enrich the heavily farmed land, while various chemicals are used to minimize damage done by insects and other pests. These chemicals are poisonous, and must be used with great care.

A tractor

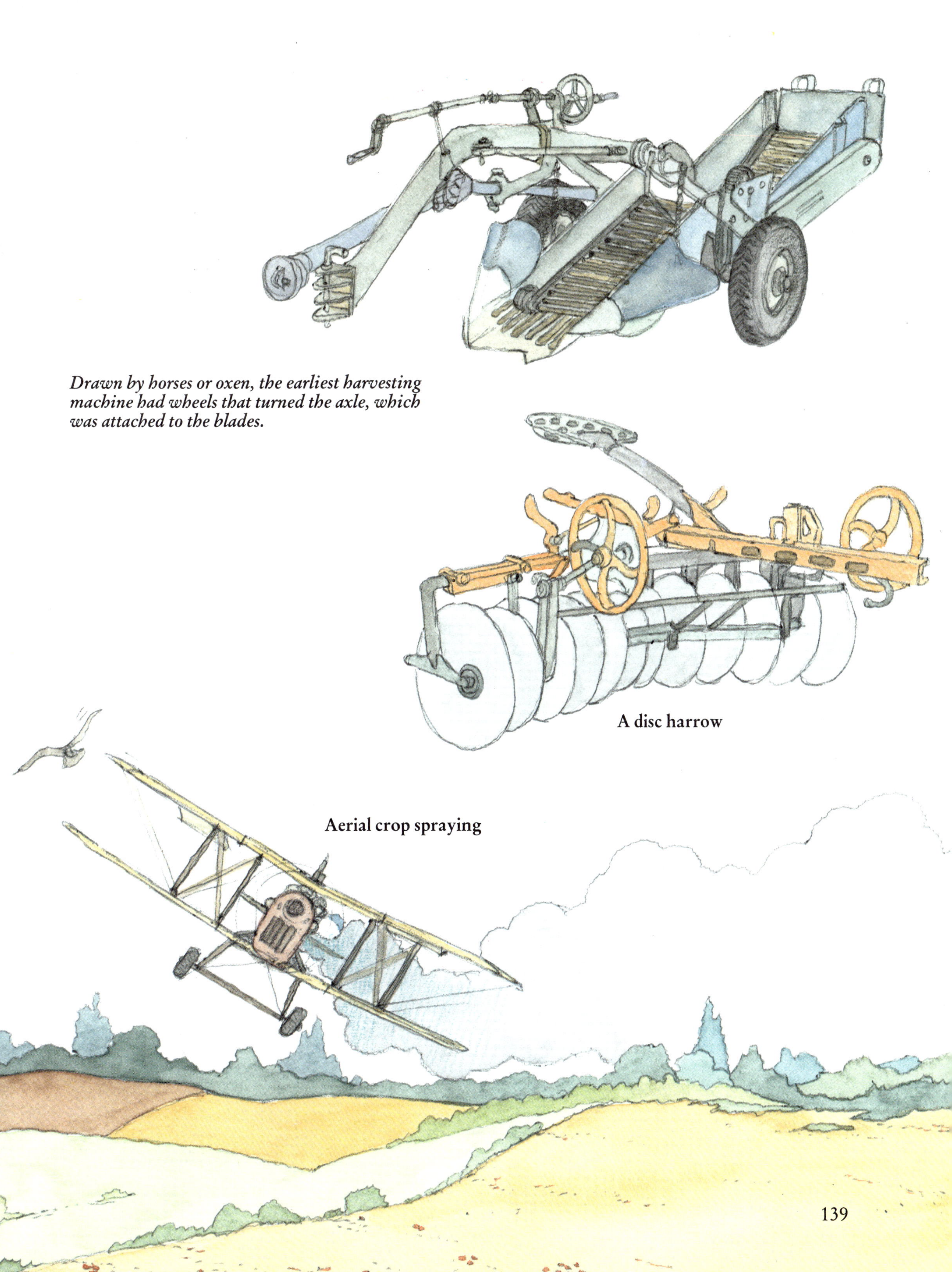

Drawn by horses or oxen, the earliest harvesting machine had wheels that turned the axle, which was attached to the blades.

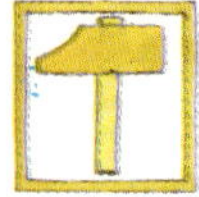

By the beginning of the 20th century, many machines were already powered by electric or internal-combustion engines. Nobody worried about running out of petrol, nor did anybody consider the problem of pollution caused by fuel-powered machinery and vehicles. In many places electricity was produced by hydroelectric power stations; efficient distribution of this 'clean energy' made it possible to set up industrial plants in almost any location.

Workshops and factories became completely mechanized and the work was divided into individual jobs, each of which was given to a certain group of workers. Although a degree of skill was still required, especially in the manufacture of luxury goods, most factories needed assembly-line work. Now workers mechanically performed the same operation over and over, day in and day out, and did not feel that the finished product was related to their particular task. But this was the only way goods could be produced cheaply enough to be made available to everyone, so that although work itself was less satisfying, there was the satisfaction of increased spending power. With the help of advertising, which whets the appetite for luxuries as well as necessities, we have become a consumer society.

Even today, skilled or semi-skilled labour is still needed in such industries as the building trade, where prefabrication and assembly-line methods are not generally used. As a result, houses are very expensive in relation to other commodities, such as mass-produced cars.

Industry needed people who were not only good manual workers, but who were able to think. A whole new work-force of technicians and administrators came into being. The latest major development of automation is the computer. This has reduced the need for workers even more than the mechanical devices used before.

The motor car industry

Because photographic enlargement processes had rot yet been perfected, a giant camera was made specially to produce this huge photograph of the joining of the two sections of the transcontinental railway in Utah.

An oil refinery

As the internal-combustion engine came into wider use, oil became a vital source of energy. Oil represented five per cent of the total energy consumption at the start of this century and 20 per cent by the 1930s. At this time natural gas began to be tapped, not so much for power as for heat.

Europe, which depended entirely on African and Middle Eastern countries for all its oil, made many of these countries into colonies or dominions, using European capital to build wells there. Most tankers carrying oil to Europe came from the Arab world, making the Suez Canal of strategic importance.

The development of merchant shipping throughout this century has been great, starting with the change-over to steam. With steamship tonnage increasing tenfold, the Atlantic crossing became safer, quicker and more comfortable. This helped to encourage a new wave of emigration to the United States.

Forty years after the first railway line was laid, Europe had 97,200 kilometres of track, with almost the same distance of track in both the United States and Canada. By the first decade of the 20th century, the figures had risen considerably.

The improvement in transport went with the development of international trade, which tripled in volume between 1870 and 1913. Throughout the 19th century, the bulk of world trade had been under British control. But by the beginning of World War I, the United States, France and Germany had become close competitors. London remained the hub of the complex exchange system and the centre of international banking.

Foreign investments and financial aid to less developed countries were decided in London. In exchange for aid, rights to exploit resources such as oil were negotiated. All this changed during the Great Depression of the 1930s.

The year after the Suez Canal opened in 1869, about 400,000
tonnes of goods passed through. By 1913, the year before
World War I, this figure had risen to about 20 million tonnes.

The drilling and commercial use of oil gave birth to the
petrochemical industry, which not only converted crude oil
into fuel, but also introduced by-products such as plastics and
synthetic fibres.

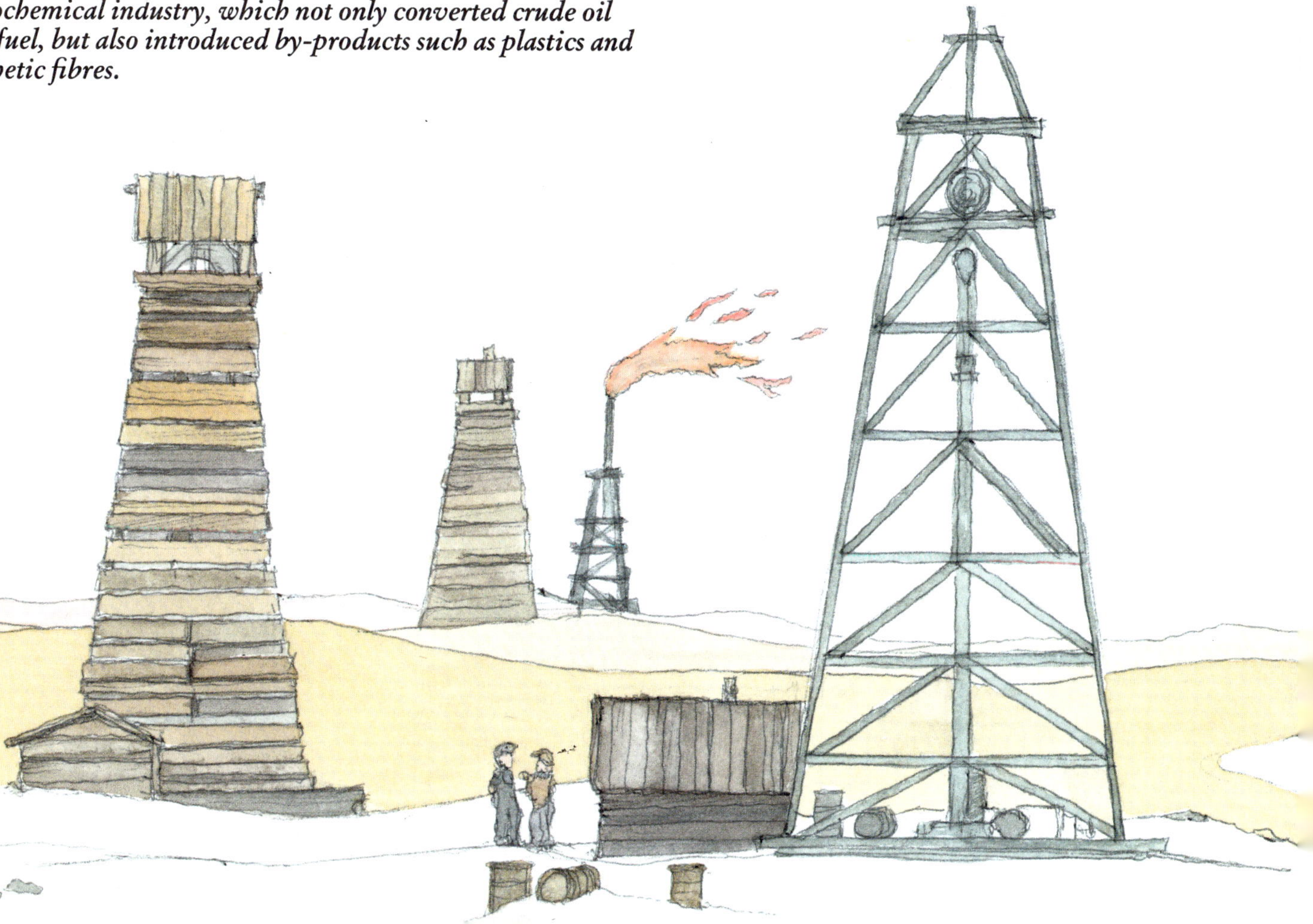

The *art nouveau* of the turn of the century was the last fanciful fling of traditional styles in dress. Full of light-hearted gaiety and confidence in the new century, the appropriately named *belle epoque* often copied the fashions of its leading stage and music hall stars.

Early 20th-century fashions were still 19th century in general character, although an occasional ankle appeared and some of the great swathes of material were trimmed down. Actually, 20th-century fashions as such did not really begin until after World War I – a war which marked the beginning of modern society. The knee-length skirts, worn with necklaces dangling to the knees, that appeared in the 'Roaring Twenties' would have been considered scandalous earlier, while Chanel's 'simple and extremely expensive' outfits would have seemed unnecessarily severe.

At the beginning of the century, men, with their black tailcoats and bowlers or top hats, seemed to be dressed permanently in mourning. Their overcoats, made of a variety of materials and colours, showed more imagination. The middle classes presented an austere image; the sober quality of their clothes suggested solid bank balances. The typical *belle epoque* male was tall and well built, with a moustache or beard. Then the American Mr Gillette patented his razor blade.

Women's accessories were many and elaborate and included bags, parasols and huge hats with feathers and flowers. Male 'swells' were fancily turned out too, with top hats, silver-knobbed canes and silver cigarette cases. The children of the day dressed almost like miniature adults.

With the commercial development of the internal-combustion engine, the great age of travel and transport began. A wide variety of machines flooded the market, from the two-wheel pedal vehicles with engines, which had appeared in the 19th century as mechanical curiosities, to the earliest motorized coaches of 1885. Then, in the first decades of the 20th century, came the mass-produced Fords. A major innovation was the use of tyres, made possible by the developments in the rubber industry.

World War I provided powerful incentives for research into both ships and flying machines. Battleships and submarines appeared on the war scene; but flight was the great adventure. Lighter-than-air gas balloons were built into rigid aerodynamically designed frames that could be operated easily and could even fly across the Atlantic Ocean.

Aeroplanes, which were faster and easier to manoeuvre than balloons, developed so rapidly that they became a formidable element in World War I. For a long time in the early days of flight seaplanes were more popular than aeroplanes because there were so few landing strips. After World War I, when the aeroplane's body was strengthened and light but powerful engines were mounted, aircraft began to be mass-produced. With these improvements, they became a reliable, and above all useful, means of transport, capable of flying 190 kilometres an hour and travelling almost 1000 kilometres per flight.

After World War I, the craze for record breaking began. The most famous feat was Charles Lindbergh's flight from New York to Paris in May, 1927. His achievement opened the possibility of a regular service between North America and Europe.

Most famous of all the airships were those built by Count Ferdinand Zeppelin in Germany and by General Umberto Nobile in Italy. After his dangerous 1926 expedition to the North Pole in the **Norge,** *Nobile tried again two years later in the* **Italia.** *This second flight ended in failure when the airship broke up on the return journey.*

The first submarine was **Nautilus** *built by the American inventor Fulton at the beginning of the 19th century. Its evolution was such that a century later during World War I the military of all countries adopted it.*

Seaplane

During World War I, tens of
thousands of flying machines were
built. Their engines were similar to
car engines, and they were
constructed with everyday
materials such as wood and oilskin,
with steel tie-rods holding the
structure together.

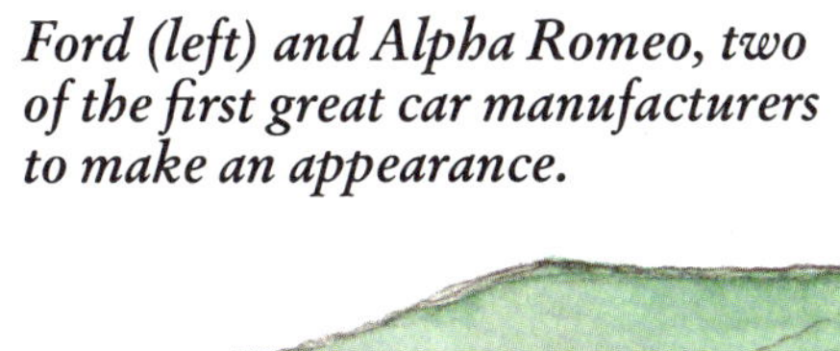

Bicycle

Motorcycle

Ford (left) and Alpha Romeo, two
of the first great car manufacturers
to make an appearance.

Antonio Pacinotti's research into the field of electromagnetism led to the invention of the dynamo. The dynamo produced electricity and used *alternators* to obtain an alternating current and *transformers* to increase the voltage or change the current. Only a high-voltage alternating current can be carried by a conductor without losing a lot of energy. To make the rotors turn around the magnet, that is to set the turbine going, oil-fuelled internal combustion engines were used. The same principle is still followed today in electric power stations, although on a far larger scale.

Distribution of electric current for lighting requires a simple, easily managed 'receiver'. This can be an arc lamp, like the ones used in some film projectors, a filament light bulb, originally invented by Thomas Edison in 1879, or a fluorescent bulb, which works by the agitation of gases as the current passes through.

The conquest of the sky really began in 1903, with Orville and Wilbur Wright's first motor-powered flight on the coast of North Carolina. Tens of thousands of aircraft were to be in the sky only fifteen years later. Jet planes, which were invented in the 1940s, have now largely replaced the old propeller type.

Among the great achievements of our century has been the development of communication by means of electromagnetic waves. Guglielmo Marconi, who had already transmitted a radio signal in 1895, was experimenting with radar by 1926. Since World War II, radios and televisions have brought new forms of information and entertainment into the home, and although the quality of reception was not always perfect at first, both media were immediate successes. Science and technology have produced countless developments – both helpful and destructive. For example, advances in microbiology have given the world vaccines against numerous diseases. But the nuclear reactor, developed in 1942, to harness a new form of energy, was used for the first time in World War II (1939–1945) in the form of the atomic bomb.

On 17 December, 1903, with Orville Wright steering and his brother Wilbur running along behind, the first aircraft took off.

After the first models were produced by the German inventor Gottlieb Daimler, motorcycles quickly evolved into something very similar to their present form, with air-cooled engines and chain drives.

The first radio broadcasts of popular music after World War I marked the beginning of a new era in entertainment.

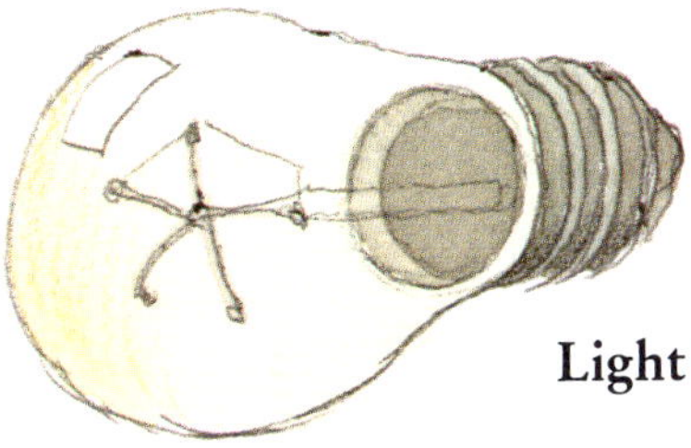

Light bulb

The famous transatlantic liner Titanic which on her maiden voyage struck an iceberg and sank.

The formation of national states continued up until World War I. This war was caused in part by economic problems and in part by Austria and Germany's hunger for power. Several million lives were lost and boys barely seventeen years old were sent to the front lines. National armies were made up of male citizens around the age of twenty who were conscripted into the army by means of a compulsory draft system.

Naval power had increased considerably, and the air corps became a third armed force, but the bulk of the vast national armies was still the infantry. The cavalry was abandoned altogether in favour of motorized vehicles: vans, jeeps, trucks, motorcycles and armoured tanks.

Battle techniques changed too. Aircraft would be the first to bombard enemy lines, tanks and then infantry would follow and heavy artillery provided back-up fire.

German infantryman and an Italian *alpino*

Italian marksman   **New Zealand officer**   **Belgian infantryman**   **French cavalryman**

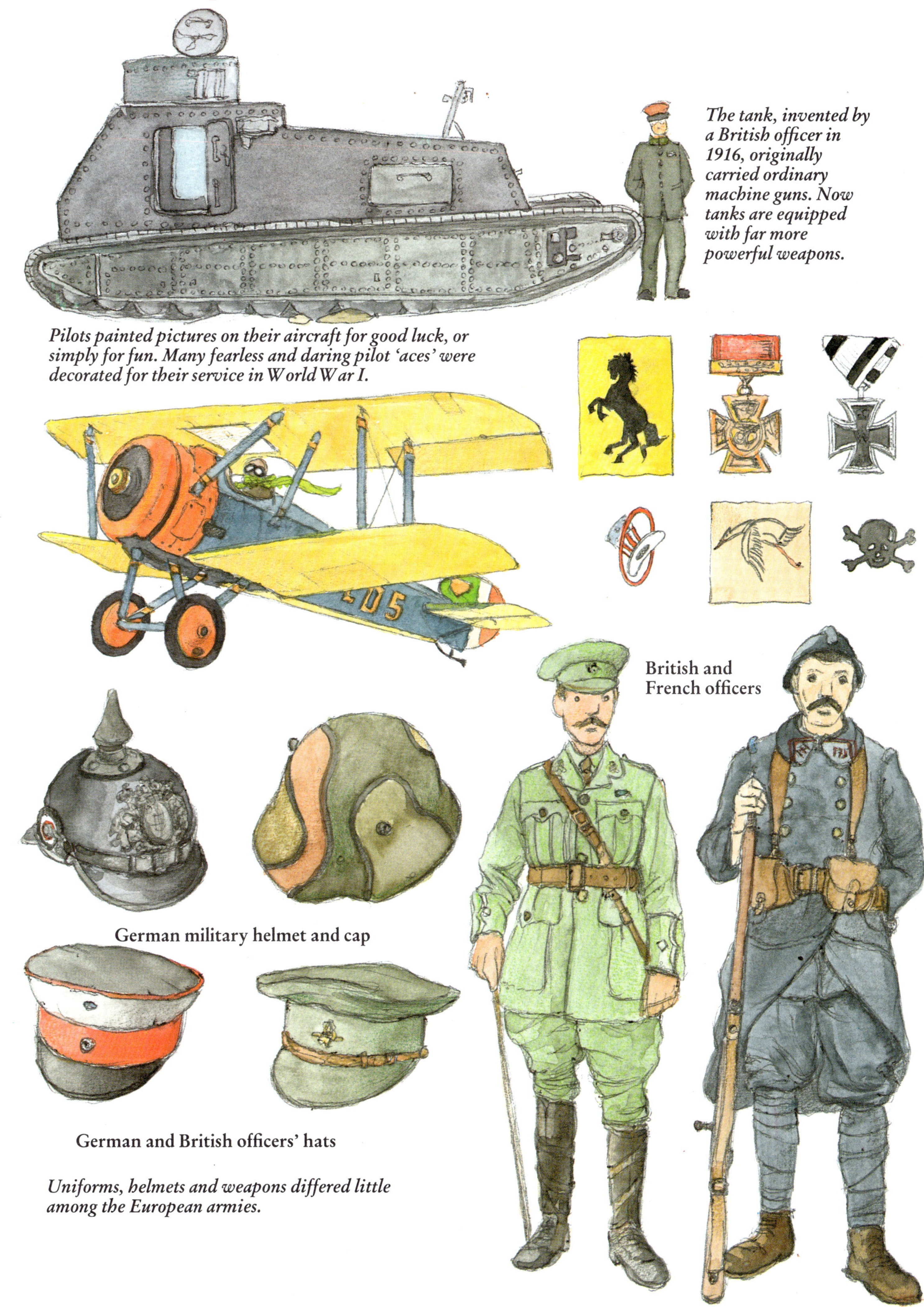

The tank, invented by a British officer in 1916, originally carried ordinary machine guns. Now tanks are equipped with far more powerful weapons.

Pilots painted pictures on their aircraft for good luck, or simply for fun. Many fearless and daring pilot 'aces' were decorated for their service in World War I.

British and French officers

German military helmet and cap

German and British officers' hats

Uniforms, helmets and weapons differed little among the European armies.

Notes

THE ANCIENT WORLD
This chapter covers the period from the dawn of history to the Hellenistic age when Greek civilization spread around the countries of the Mediterranean. Hellenism followed the conquests of Alexander the Great, who died in 323 BC, leaving his empire to the generals who had helped to create it.

The chronology of the ancient empires can easily be looked up in history books. The emphasis in this chapter is on the period of the closer contact between those ancient civilizations which occurred towards the end of the second millennium BC. About that time the Hittite empire broke up, while in Mesopotamia there was a succession of ruling dynasties, starting with the Sumerians and ending with the Persians, who emerged as a power in the second half of the first millennium BC, with the growth of Greek cities. The civilization which left the greatest mark on the history of the western world in terms of language, art, philosophy and scientific thought is that of Greece. The Hebrew tradition is of great religious and moral importance; it was from this tradition that the Christian religion sprang.

Burial   It seems certain that the earliest Mediterranean people buried their dead. After the invasions of Nordic peoples cremation became common. The two types of funeral custom suggest two different primitive religious tendencies, one towards the earth as mother of all living things, to which every being returns after death; the other towards the light-filled sky, towards which the smoke of the pyres rises, accompanying the spirit of the dead person.

Worship   In the world of the first nomads worship was very much concerned with the stars and their movements. From this observation of the sky was established the cycle of nomadic migrations. To this day we measure time by certain regular astronomical phenomena such as the rotation of the earth (day), the phases of the moon (weeks), the revolution of the moon (month), the equinoxes and solstices (seasons), the revolution of the earth (year). This rhythm is still marked by festivals, such as Sunday and New Year.

When the wandering tribes settled and they turned to working the land, worship began to centre around the production of crops and animals, in short, fertility. Mother Earth became the most important divinity. A mixture of the two great religious expressions (Earth and Sky) is found in Greek mythology, which is based on religious stories (myths) and religious practices (rites).

Crops   Grain was the basic food of the ancient peoples. The various types of grain (wheat, barley, oats, millet, sesame), are rich in proteins, vitamins and oils. So, not surprisingly, farming in these civilizations revolved largely around these products, especially since they could be stored. Fruit and vegetables were luxuries, and in particular citrus fruits: only kings had orange groves.

Meat was eaten only after the entrails of the animal had been burned in honour of the gods. Various aromatic herbs were added to make their offerings acceptable. This is the origin of cooking meat with rosemary, sage, bay-leaves and other herbs, which also cover any unpleasant smells.

Pottery   'Terracotta' – which means in Latin 'cooked earth' – is a basic clay, modelled and dried in ovens. Fine white clay such as kaolin was later used, to make the delicate yet strong type of ceramics known as porcelain. Porcelain was first made in China.

Styles of decoration changed with historical periods. The naturalistic style was typical of Crete and the geometric style of 'archaic' Greece. The two best-known Greek styles use red and black. The first uses black figures on red (the figure is painted in black on a red background); the other uses red figures on a black background. One style can be thought of, in film terms, as the positive of the other's negatives.

Metals   After the Stone Age, ancient historical periods are named after the metals that were most commonly used. Copper, a soft metal which is easy to smelt, gives its name to the first of the ages; this is followed by the Bronze Age. Bronze, being a mixture of copper and tin requires a knowledge of alloys. The last metal age is the Iron Age. Iron is a metal with a very high melting point and is therefore more difficult to obtain. This system of dating by metal use is used for dating civilizations in different parts of the world. It does not mean, of course, that other metals such as lead, gold and silver were not known at the same time. Although easy to smelt and work, some of the metals, such as gold, were not easy to find. At first gold was obtained from sandy river beds.

Glass Glass was probably discovered when people noticed that the sand over which the metals were smelted, dissolved and cooled to become a compact, semi-transparent paste. This paste could be moulded when it was still hot. Glass-making was highly developed in Syrian cities in the first centuries before Christ: workshops were already experimenting with the technique of glass-blowing, to obtain hollow containers such as vases.

Trade The Cretans are mentioned on an Egyptian inscription of the New Kingdom as paying tribute to the Pharaoh with many products. These may not in fact have been tributes, but rather records of the trade which the Cretans carried on along the coast of the Mediterranean. The Phoenicians were as much renowned as merchants as they were navigators. One of their most prized products was a purple dye obtained from a mollusc *(murex)*. Their other national product was cedar wood, from the mountains of Lebanon. This wood was used in building Solomon's temple in Jerusalem.

Apart from trade, there were also cultural exchanges between peoples. Each year to the beaches of the Phoenician city of Byblos, the head of the Egyptian god, Osiris, was borne over the sea. In myth, Osiris was killed and hacked to pieces by the demon Seth. The women of Byblos performed the ritual of carrying the head to the temple and began a great celebration. It was in fact the goddess Isis who, through her love, once again gave life to her lamented husband.

Cities Excavation work on Syrian cities such as Ugarit and Ebla gives us a clear idea of the layout of the ancient city-states. They had an acropolis, or high city, the fortified site of the temple and palace. At the foot were the people's dwellings, set along streets and squares. Still further down the hill the city was protected by another circle of walls.

Cloth The most commonly used material in Egypt was a kind of linen obtained from the fibres of the flax grown along the banks of the Nile. In Greece most material was made from sheep's wool. The fibres were spun and twisted by hand by the women, but both men and women have always been involved in the making of clothes.

Boats We know very little about Cretan and Phoenician ships. From the historian Herodotus, we learn that at the battle of Salamis (480 BC) the Persians attacked with a powerful fleet, while the Greeks (the victors) had a fleet of 378 ships. Older evidence about Greek ships is to be found in Homer's poems.

Roads The greatest road builders of antiquity, before the Romans, were undoubtedly the Persians. The only really good Greek roads were the 'processional' ones, which led to great shrines. The road from Athens to the shore of Elat was about 30 kilometres long. The idea of processional roads leading to shrines is echoed to the present day, in pilgrimage routes.

Technology In antiquity all technology, particularly metallurgy, was regarded as a semi-divine skill and was therefore a closely guarded secret. Prometheus was the demi-god who tamed fire, and Hephaestus the god who made the weapons for heroes. In reality metals were traded from special jealously-guarded centres of production, either in ingots, like copper, or in ready-shaped objects, such as iron goods.

Writing The deciphering of Babylonian cuneiform and Egyptian hieroglyphic writing was made possible only by means of documents written in several languages of which one at least was already known. The Rosetta stone is a good instance of this: on it the same text was repeated in Egyptian hieroglyphs, everyday Egyptian and Greek script. This stone was seized by the French during Napoleon's Egyptian campaign in 1798. It was deciphered by Jean-François Champollion.

Weapons In ancient times the losses in human life were small in comparison with the booty to be gained. Wars were decided mostly in combat between armies, without any serious harm to the civilian population. A war chariot drawn by two horses could spread terror among the enemy ranks without doing very much damage. A soldier might die from a minor wound, for there were no medicines to prevent infection. Strong infusions of herbs were used to alleviate pain.

IMPERIAL ROME

This chapter deals with the Roman Empire at the height of its power and expansion around AD 100. The Roman Empire was founded by Octavian Augustus at the end of the civil wars, in 26 BC. It lasted in the West until AD 476, when the last emperor, Romulus Augustulus was deposed.

The emperor Trajan (AD 98–117) carried out a series of military campaigns to extend and strengthen the borders of the empire to the north and east. His exploits are immortalized in the bas-reliefs of Trajan's column, put up in his honour in Rome. Under his successor, Hadrian, came a period of peace. It marked an era of great prosperity throughout the provinces, the regions administered by the Romans.

Cities   Roman cities were very orderly. This order was not only functional, it was also concerned with religious rituals. Before siting the city centre – the crossing of the two main axes – the surveyors consulted the augurs or soothsayers who would then perform special rites. They watched for omens in, for example, the flight of birds.

Architecture and the figurative arts   Scholars talk about the Romans' eclecticism in art and about their ability to take various ideas and techniques from different artistic traditions, whether Greek or Etruscan. They nevertheless developed certain building styles and inventions of their own. The amphitheatre, basilica and baths are buildings which have no exact equivalent in other civilizations. The Roman fondness for round forms (the arch, cylinder and dome) is typical. In sculpture and painting too they introduced realism, in contrast to the Greeks who tended to idealize the human figure according to laws of perfection more suited to the representation of the gods than ordinary mortals.

Despite its monumental forms and decorations, Roman architecture was always functional. Referring to the aqueducts, a senator is said to have commented 'These are our pyramids'.

Land reclamation   In founding colonies, the Romans often chose marshy or barren land, and carried out large-scale works of reclamation. Examples of these operations can be seen today in the Po valley, at the mouth of the Rhône in France, and around Cambridge in England.

Public works   Detailed records, etched on bronze tablets, were kept about the subdivision of urban land into building lots and of the countryside into cultivable plots. These records were kept in Rome. Some lots were earmarked for the building of public works, including baths and lavatories, and sewage systems carried the waste and dirty water from the city.

The Romans were unsurpassed in the building of public works and roads. The roads bore the names of the consul under whose jurisdiction they had been made, for example, the Emilia road.

Law-making   Laws, too, bore the name of the man who had drafted them, followed by the matter they dealt with. In many countries Roman law is still studied in law faculties. It was produced by a fine balance between respect for the freedom of the individual and the demands of public institutions.

The army   The baggage waggons which accompanied the legions with supplies, tools and equipment were an easy prey for the enemy and slowed down the march. By Marius' reform of the military system in 100 BC, it was decided that the legionaries should carry all their personal baggage on their shoulders like a pack saddle. As a result legionaries became known as 'Marius' mules'.

The camp was drawn up according to a precise plan. The administrative buildings and commander's house (General Staff) were in the centre, and the barracks at the sides. The defence works were about thirty metres from the barracks, to avoid their being struck by missiles.

Iron discipline held the legion together. Victory in combat was well rewarded, but punishment for any lack of discipline was severe. Anyone turning tail before the enemy was whipped until blood flowed; deserters were executed. The legion's ensign was never allowed to leave the camp.

The navy   During imperial times there were four permanent fleets, two in Italy (at Cuma near Naples, and at Ravenna), one on the North Sea and one on the Black Sea.

THE FIRST MILLENNIUM

The period dealt with in this chapter extends over the centuries which saw the reorganization of a hard-won new social and political order in Europe after the fall of the Roman empire. Because of the fragmentation of the forces which invaded the empire, it was difficult for any Germanic chieftains to keep such vast territories and such an assortment of peoples under control. When the campaign for the reconquest of Italy was launched from Byzantium (capital of the eastern Roman empire), initial successes were considerable. But Byzantium itself had its own problems in the east and could not become embroiled in the defence of the west. The Ostrogoths followed by the Franks preferred to seek a reconciliation with the Roman world. This was confirmed by the mass conversion to Christianity and the agreements with the Pope, the only authority who could officially sanction new central power. Thus was born the Holy Roman Empire. For Rome the price of this political operation was her final split with the Orthodox Church of the East.

The fief   The German empire was subdivided into 'fiefs' (territorial and political units). This system was adopted by the emperor, and then the king in France and England. When the fief became hereditary, aristocracy was formed which was often in conflict with the central power. This created serious dynastic problems, along with political and military tensions.

The 'heavenly city'   During these troubled times the idea of the 'heavenly city' arose, a place where freedom and equality would be the aim of all men in a just and upright society. The symbol of this ideal city was the monastery, where the values of discipline, hard work and mutual respect were honoured. So the monastery had a great influence on the formation of medieval cities.

The Romanesque   In art, the style which became widespread in buildings, and carved or painted decoration was the Romanesque (or in England, Norman): from Roman taste it retained a certain grandeur (as in the basilicas) and a love of realism, while from the oriental tradition it took a feeling for colour (glowing mosaics, for example), minute detail, and a certain static quality. Lastly, the 'barbarian' world added a primitive and spontaneous feeling for creativity.

The fair   The fair as a trading centre was one of the reasons for the development and wealth of the medieval city. The most important fairs, large-scale markets set up on special occasions, were linked to religious festivals with large gatherings of people. On such occasions trade was tax-free and was conducted according to its own negotiating laws on the basis of the supply and demand of certain goods.

Saddle and stirrup   In the ancient world people did not ride bareback; a covering was used, possibly of hide. The Germanic tribes considered such a covering to be a sign of softness. But real saddles made their appearance among the Romans as late as the 4th century AD.

The rigid metal stirrup is seen for the first time in Europe in the Hungarian tombs of the Avars, horsemen who came from the steppes of Asia around AD 560. In northern Europe the stirrup appears in the 8th century. Before the stirrup, horsemen used leather rings to support their feet, but these were clearly not efficient.

THE MIDDLE AGES

This chapter deals with the period around 1200, when medieval society reached its period of greatest splendour. One of the causes that brought about its eventual decline was the Black Death, which raged throughout Europe for about 20 years in the first half of the 14th century.

Population   Here we look at data which will give us an idea of the increase in population which occurred after the year 1000 until the Black Death. In 1086 there were 1,200,000 people living in the English shires, and in 1340 there were 2,355,000, practically double the number. In the particularly rich and fertile German region between the Rhine and the Moselle, the population increased tenfold between the 10th and 13th centuries. In four centuries, in Germany, at least 2500 towns came into existence, some of which were to become the great cities we know today.

City growth was widespread. In 1200 Paris had about 100,000 inhabitants, which swelled to 240,000 by 1300. The small island on the Seine, the *Lutetia Parisiorum* of the Romans, became a great capital. Florence too, doubled in size in the same period, and so did the Flemish cities of Bruges and Ghent. The rights which the individual communes on the continent demanded and obtained from the central authorities were the following: the right to hold a market regularly; the right to devise their own systems of weights and measures; the right to try their own citizens in local courts according to their own laws; and the right to bear arms.

Civil guard   Bodies of armed men were needed to defend the cities and to keep order. All male citizens, apart from those in religious orders, had to serve in the civil guard. Many towns also had a night-watch.

Cathedrals and churches   More than any other monument, cathedrals expressed the degree of economic and technological development of a medieval society. It also symbolized the central position occupied by Christianity in the Middle Ages. The Church was a focal point. These splendid cathedrals were used mainly on great festivals; the day to-day religious life revolved around the small parish churches. To this day medieval towns have dozens of small churches and chapels.

Public services   The Church was a complex organization. Its presence was felt in all town activities. It was particularly concerned with all works of charity – from lodging pilgrims in hospices to caring for the sick in hospitals. In this way society was relieved of these unproductive and expensive duties. Unlike the fatalism of the pagan world which did not care about the sick, old and suffering, Christianity valued suffering for its own sake and at the same time commended those who helped to look after those who suffered.

Guilds The Middle Ages had a corporate economy, one based on the association of people who practised the same activity. The guilds favoured the development of their own trade in art, for the benefit of all. But they were rigid in structure with sharp distinctions between apprentices, journeymen and masters who themselves were ranked in order of seniority. The merchants' meeting-place (the guild hall) might have two rooms for the weddings of their members, one first class and one second class. Capitalism was in a sense founded on the guilds, notably in that they recognized the importance of wealth invested in labour. The bosses were masters in their own craft or trade and did not regard manual work as demeaning. Only the feudal aristocracy did not work – unless hunting and bearing arms could be counted as such.

Universities One of the most important medieval institutions was the University. Law, based on Roman law, was particularly important, so too was medicine, which revived the medical tradition of the Greeks and Arabs; and, above all, theology, where the Christian vision was interpreted by St Thomas Aquinas. Among the oldest universities were Bologna (1100), Paris (1150), Oxford (1170) and Salamanca (1243). Many scholars travelled from one university to another.

Water power This description of the river running through the abbey at Clairvaux in France may give an idea of the uses of this source of energy: 'The river enters the abbey through a conduit. It follows first to the mill, where its power is used to turn the mighty wheels which grind the grain and operate the sifter which separates the flour from the bran. The river flows into a nearby building and fills the vats in which the monks' beer is brewed-…Then it flows to the fulling machines just beyond the millhouse. In the mill it helped to prepare the monks' food while here it helps to make the habits they wear…The river then flows to the tannery, where its water devotes much effort and care preparing the leather for the monks'

sandals. It then divides into many small streams and, on its busy way, seeks out those who require its services for whatever purpose, cooking, turning, crushing, watering, washing and so on. Finally, to earn the fullest thanks and so that nothing shall be left undone, it carries away the refuse and leaves everything well and truly clean.'

ABSOLUTE MONARCHS
This chapter deals with the centuries between the 15th and 17th, when the absolute power of the reigning dynasties was consolidated, and when the free cities developed into dukedoms.

The Republics The Republic of Venice, up to now devoted entirely to maritime trade, extended its territories inland and established dominions overseas. As long as maritime interests were concentrated in the Mediterranean, Venice continued to increase its power, triumphantly defeating the Saracens and setting up settlements in Crete, Cyprus and other strategic islands. But with the opening up of the Atlantic routes, another republic, that of Holland, was to rule the seas. The 17th century was the golden age of Dutch economic and cultural development. After a long and hard struggle to gain independence from Spain, the seven provinces of the Low Countries united and set up their own republic. Here the burghers became the ruling class. The city of Amsterdam, from being a small port on the Amstel on an inland sea, grew to become a great capital, whose planned development was the finest example of town-planning in history.

Renaissance This is a term which describes the great period of cultural revival which affected all branches of study and the arts from 1400 onwards. It is linked to Humanism, a rediscovery of the Greco-Roman world in philosophy and literature. In Florence, within a few decades, three great artists, Brunelleschi, Donatello and Masaccio gave new life to architecture, sculpture and painting.

The navigators The new burst of cultural life and man's new-found faith in himself contributed largely to the successes in the discovery of new continents. The spirit of adventure led brave men to cross the oceans and indeed, with Magellan, to sail around the world.

The galley, sailing ship and galleon The galley was the traditional warship of the Mediterranean.

It had between 25 and 80 benches on each side and each bench seated three oarsmen, each with a separate oar. It had a single mast with a lateen sail, so that the oarsmen could rest when a favourable wind was blowing. The oarsmen were usually criminals or prisoners of war. They were chained to their bench throughout the voyage and were urged on with wine and the whip. Small galleys were called galliots, brigantines and frigates.

The mercantile galley was larger and could carry up to 250 tonnes of merchandise. It had three masts and used oars only in emergency. In its bows it had cannons. It was regarded as being so safe that merchants could avoid insuring their goods.

The Mediterranean galley was unsuited to Atlantic waters. There, ships with round hulls were used, which could carry men and provisions for the long voyage. The masts had several sails – not so that it could better catch the wind, but because a variety of smaller sails made them easier to control, as well as safer in the open sea. The ships on which Columbus and Magellan sailed on their historic voyages were really most unsuitable. A contemporary wrote in 1518, of the five ships acquired in Spain for the circumnavigation of the world: 'They are very old and patched up, and I would not willingly travel on them even to the Canary Islands, because their sides are as soft as butter'.

The galleon had been developed by the Portuguese as a large warship. This model was used by the Spanish and English to build their powerful fleets, which were to clash in the Channel in the Armada of 1588. The galleon was armed with heavy cannon and was swift, despite its considerable tonnage.

Fashion   In 16th century Italy, the double, interchangeable sleeve for one single garment was the fashion. People sometimes had many pairs of sleeves, which could be put on to several garments. This allowed for different combinations and gave rise to the Italian expression 'That's another pair of sleeves', meaning 'quite a different matter'. Sleeves and stockings were sometimes slit to reveal linings in brightly coloured silk through the slits.

Gunpowder   Gunpowder was known in Europe from the 13th century. It is a mixture of saltpetre, sulphur and charcoal. It was invented in China and brought to Europe possibly via Byzantium. The application of gunpowder to firearms was a European invention. The mixture was made with a pestle and mortar and the powder was kept damp to avoid accidental explosions.

Soldiers of fortune   In the 16th century bands of mercenaries, led by adventurous captains, were professionals of war. They chose the flag which paid the most money.

Fortifications   The use of gunpowder and new weapons brought about changes in military engineering. Cities could no longer be defended by towers and walls, so powerful ramparts were built.

THE AGE OF REVOLUTION
Here we look at the 18th century, the 'age of enlightenment'.

Great Britain   Throughout the 18th century England was the testing-ground for developments in trade, agriculture and industry. Whole series of experiments were carried out here in the various fields of technology and production. Because of its widespread use of steam engines, Great Britain became the leader in the industrial revolution.

The Lunar Society   Towards the end of the 18th century, a strange society was founded in Birmingham in England. Among its members were scientific thinkers and industrialists, inventors and scholars. Matthew Boulton, James Watt, Erasmus Darwin (grandfather of Charles), Josiah Wedgwood, the potter and William Herschel, the astronomer, were counted among the members. The name *Lunar Society* came from the fact that the group met every month on the Monday nearest to the full moon when, having met and dined in the evening, they could return home by moonlight.

The date of a meeting was announced in this strange way: 'You are reminded that the next full moon will be Saturday March 3rd.' With little or no publicity, this group of industrialists, inventors and philosophers helped to transform science and technology in Britain.

'Off-the-peg' clothes   Post-Revolutionary Paris was the home of fashion and elegance. The first shops selling ready-made, cheap clothes opened there. Fashions were in danger of becoming no more than a passing fad. There was a serious risk of unemployment for many classes of workers, and the loss of a valuable tradition of craftsmanship. This resulted in the development of a new fashion of 'haute couture' during the time of Napoleon, which was largely inspired by paintings by the artist, David, depicting scenes from the Roman world. This was why the new clothes fashion became known as the Empire style.

THE AGE OF PROGRESS

The 19th century was the age of coal and steel, of industrial production and the railways. It was a time when great hopes were placed in the use of the machine.

The Risorgimento   One of the most important movements for national unity and liberation from foreign powers was the Italian Risorgimento. This gave Italy the impetus to regain its nationhood after so many centuries. This period saw the wars of independence against the Austro-Hungarian empire, which was occupying Lombardy and the Veneto, and also the famous 'Expedition of the Thousand', led by Giuseppe Garibaldi to reunite the south with the north. This renunion was sealed by the capture of Rome in 1870.

Slum clearance   In the 19th century crumbling, dirty town centres were razed in a massive 'slum clearance' exercise. The avowed aim was to clear away unhealthy, insanitary districts. But these operations were often clumsily carried out, and destroyed whole neighbourhoods without actually solving the housing problem.

Impressionism   There was a revolution in art, in the second half of the century. There emerged a new movement, contemptuously known as 'Impressionism'. The first exhibitions of painters whom we today regard as geniuses, such as Renoir and Manet, were attended by people who went there to mock, or express their outrage. With Impressionism, modern art was born.

Feminism   In all fields, 19th century ideas expressed a tendency towards renewal and a demand for freedom and justice. Women, too, began to speak out against their state of subjection and above all their exclusion from places of learning and public life. In fashion, as early as the Romantic period, a group of women, the Lionesses, were following the style of dress of Georges Sand, a female writer who used this masculine name, and who often wore men's clothing. These were the forerunners of the suffragettes, though in fact 'universal suffrage' was achieved much later.

THE TURN OF THE CENTURY

Futurism   In all fields, the first decade of the 20th century revealed a passionate desire for change as well as great optimism for the future. The cultural movement which particularly expressed this spirit was 'Futurism', with its exaltation of speed, the machine and great human undertaking.

But there were also stirrings of doubt and unease expressed by other phiolosophical and artistic movements, such as French and German Expressionism. Here there was a more critical awareness – in Europe at least – and a widespread fear that progress also carried within it the seeds of destruction and death. The great European tragedy of the two world wars forced people to think again about the limits of development, and to think of planning the future in more rational terms.

Architecture   War damage involved architects and engineers in large-scale works of reconstruction. The massive movement into the towns provided a strong incentive to seek alternative solutions to mere haphazard expansion. Satellite 'new' towns were built to reduce concentration in the great cities, and there were plans to design 'linear cities' along the great roads and railways.

The movement which dominated architectural planning and urban design in the 20th century was 'Rationalism' – for it tended towards a rational and functional solution of the housing problem.

Energy   Internal combustion engines were at first used to produce electrical energy. They worked the turbines that produced alternating current.

Another source of energy was water, used to power hydro-electric generating stations. The flow of water in canals and waterfalls was a renewable and theoretically inexhaustible source. It was free and did not pollute.

The disadvantage of hydro-electric power stations is that they had to be built where geographical conditions dictated – near waterfalls and so on. Lines had to be laid over great distances and at great expense to transport the current. There was therefore a shift to thermo-electric stations fuelled by oil. They can be built anywhere and the fuel can be stored.

Because oil as a source of fuel may be exhausted in the next few decades, many European countries have begun to build nuclear power-stations, which make use of atomic energy.

One problem is how to produce electrical energy cheap enough so as not to affect the price of the products. It is short-sighted to allow a purely economic viewpoint to dictate in these matters, especially if the repercussions could be atmospheric pollution and radioactive contamination. We should rather be thinking of developing research into forms of alternative energy which do not pollute our environment.

Index